JEWISH
CHOICES,
JEWISH
VOICES

# WAR AND NATIONAL SECURITY

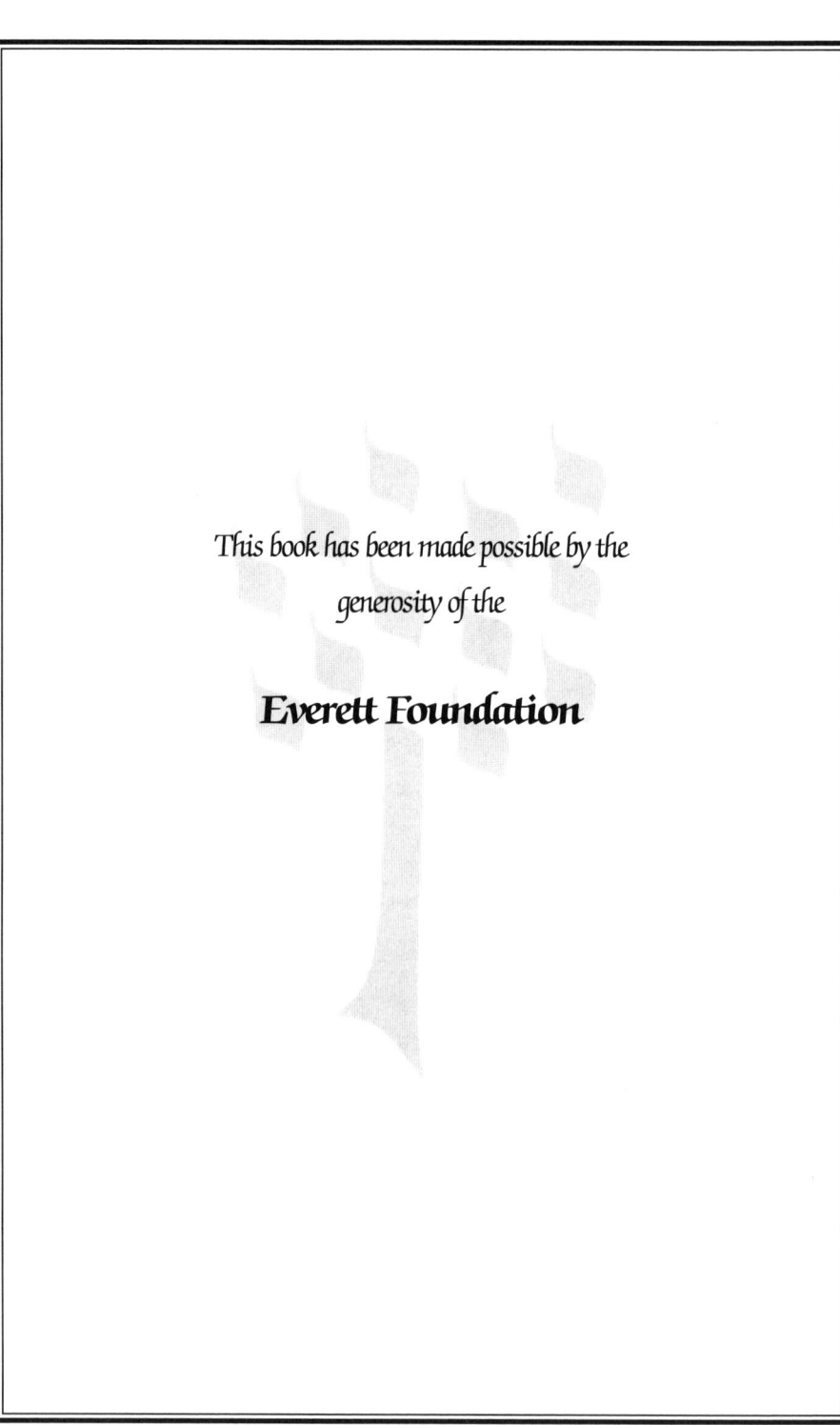

This book has been made possible by the
generosity of the

**Everett Foundation**

# Jewish Choices, Jewish Voices

# WAR AND NATIONAL SECURITY

Edited by
Elliot N. Dorff
and
Danya Ruttenberg

2010 • 5770
The Jewish Publication Society
Philadelphia

> JPS is a nonprofit educational association and the oldest and foremost publisher of Judaica in English in North America. The mission of JPS is to enhance Jewish culture by promoting the dissemination of religious and secular works, in the United States and abroad, to all individuals and institutions interested in past and contemporary Jewish life.

Copyright © 2010 by Elliot N. Dorff and Danya Ruttenberg
First edition. All rights reserved.

No part of this book may be reproduced or transmitted in any form or by any means, electronic or mechanical, including photocopy, recording, or any information storage or retrieval system, except for brief passages in connection with a critical review, without permission in writing from the publisher:

**The Jewish Publication Society**
2100 Arch Street, 2nd floor
Philadelphia, PA 19103
*www.jewishpub.org*

Design and Composition by Progressive Information Technologies
Manufactured in the United States of America

09 10 11 12   10 9 8 7 6 5 4 3 2 1
ISBN: 978–0–8276–0860–3   (v.1. BODY)
ISBN: 978–0–8276–0861–0   (v.2. MONEY)
ISBN: 978–0–8276–0862–7   (v.3. POWER)
ISBN: 978–0–8276–0905–1   (v.4. SEX AND INTIMACY)
ISBN: 978–0–8276–0906–8   (v.5. WAR AND NATIONAL SECURITY)

Library of Congress Cataloging-in-Publication Data:
Jewish choices, Jewish voices / edited by Elliot N. Dorff, Louis E. Newman. — 1st ed.
    v. cm.
    Includes bibliographical references and index.
    Contents: v. 1. Body
    ISBN 978-0-8276-0860-3 (ALK. PAPER)
    1. Jewish ethics.   2. Jews—Identity.   3. Body, Human—Religious aspects—Judaism.   I. Dorff, Elliot N.   II. Newman, Louis E.

BJ1285.2.J49 2008
296.3'6—dc22                    2007037402

---

JPS books are available at discounts for bulk purchases for reading groups, special sales, and fundraising purchases. Custom editions, including personalized covers, can be created in larger quantities for special needs. For more information, please contact us at marketing@jewishpub.org or at this address: 2100 Arch Street, Philadelphia, PA 19103.

# Contents

Acknowledgments................................................ix

Introduction....................................................xi

**CASE 1: NATIONAL SECURITY**

  Case Study................................................... 3

    Traditional Sources
    *Uzi Weingarten and the Editors*........................5

    Contemporary Sources
    *Steven Edelman-Blank*..................................8

  Responses:

    Homeland Security
    *Nadav Morag*..........................................15

    Responses to Terror and their Consequences:
    An Interview with Noam Chomsky
    *Elliot N. Dorff*......................................21

    Terrorism—A Viewpoint
    *Joan Schultz*.........................................30

    The Necessity for Strong National Security
    *Larry Greenfield*.....................................34

    Politics, Rights, and Security
    *Ben Murane*...........................................40

**CASE 2: JUSTIFICATIONS FOR WAR**

  Case Study...................................................49

    Traditional Sources
    *Uzi Weingarten and the Editors*.......................51

    Contemporary Sources
    *Steven Edelman-Blank*.................................54

  Responses:

    War in the Jewish Tradition
    *Michael Walzer*.......................................59

    From the Dream of an Ideal Society to the Reality of
    Self-Defense
    *Donna Robinson Divine*................................64

The Challenges of Using Self-Defense as a Justification
for War: An Interview with Rebecca Vilkomerson
*Elliot N. Dorff* . . . . . . . . . . . . . . . . . . . . . . . . . . . . . . . . . . . . . . . 70

CASE 3: THE CONDUCT OF WAR

Case Study. . . . . . . . . . . . . . . . . . . . . . . . . . . . . . . . . . . . . . . . . . . . .81

Traditional Sources
*Uzi Weingarten and the Editors.* . . . . . . . . . . . . . . . . . . . . . . . .83

Contemporary Sources
*Steven Edelman-Blank* . . . . . . . . . . . . . . . . . . . . . . . . . . . . . . . .85

Responses:

To Keep Our Honor Clean
*Seth M. Milstein.* . . . . . . . . . . . . . . . . . . . . . . . . . . . . . . . . . . . . .91

Fighting, with Fear and Trembling
*Sharon Brous.* . . . . . . . . . . . . . . . . . . . . . . . . . . . . . . . . . . . . . . 101

Ethics on the Battlefield
*Joe Kashnow* . . . . . . . . . . . . . . . . . . . . . . . . . . . . . . . . . . . . . . . 105

Rules for War
*Ari Brochin* . . . . . . . . . . . . . . . . . . . . . . . . . . . . . . . . . . . . . . . . 110

Does Torah Permit Torture? Defending Dignity, Life,
and Sacred Personhood
*Melissa Weintraub*. . . . . . . . . . . . . . . . . . . . . . . . . . . . . . . . . . 116

CASE 4: NATIONAL POLICIES CONCERNING WAR

Case Study. . . . . . . . . . . . . . . . . . . . . . . . . . . . . . . . . . . . . . . . . . .129

Traditional Sources
*Uzi Weingarten and the Editors.* . . . . . . . . . . . . . . . . . . . . . . 131

Contemporary Sources
*Steven Edelman-Blank* . . . . . . . . . . . . . . . . . . . . . . . . . . . . . . 135

Responses:

A Solemn Duty: Citizens' Responsibilities for the Nation's
Wars and Warriors
*Harold L. Robinson* . . . . . . . . . . . . . . . . . . . . . . . . . . . . . . . . . 140

War, Peace, and National Security: A Theme and Variations
*Linda B. Miller* . . . . . . . . . . . . . . . . . . . . . . . . . . . . . . . . . . . . 145

The Ethics of the Sale of Arms by Governments
*Steven L. Spiegel*. . . . . . . . . . . . . . . . . . . . . . . . . . . . . . . . . . . 150

The Complex Relationship between the Military and
the Economy: An Interview with Richard Immerman
*Julia Oestreich* .................................158

Conclusion: The Ethics of War and National Security ............167
Suggestions for Further Reading.............................169
Editors and Contributors ...................................173
Index  ...................................................180

# Acknowledgments

No book—let alone a series of books—comes about without the creative energy and support of many people. We wish to thank, first and foremost, Ellen Frankel, Editor Emerita of The Jewish Publication Society, for her vision in first conceiving of this series and for her willingness to entrust it to our editorship. The JPS National Council played a critical role early on as the scope and format of the series were in the development stage. Julia Oestreich was invaluable and indefatigable as the Project Manager of this volume, acting with care, thoroughness and thoughtfulness at every turn, helping us to keep track of what needed to be done, making wonderful suggestions about possible contributors, and providing us with astute and constructive comments about earlier drafts of every part of this volume, including our own writing. Along with the editors, Rabbis Uzi Weingarten and Steven Edelman-Blank collected, respectively, the classical and the contemporary Jewish sources for this volume. We are indebted to them for their fine work in locating these materials. We also wish to thank Monica Barr, Assistant Project Manager, who helped us immensely in contacting our contributors, making sure that they received and signed the proper contracts, and working with them to ensure that their contributions came in on time and that we had the latest versions of their essays in hand. We would additionally like to thank Julia Oestreich and Janet Liss for their skillful copyediting work, including organizing and coordinating scores of details necessary to ready this volume for publication. Their diligence and attention to detail are evident on every page of this book. Finally, we especially want to thank our contributors, whose creativity and thoughtfulness make this anthology the stimulating and deeply Jewish book that it is.

E.N.D.
D.R.

# Introduction

Seek peace and pursue it. *(Psalms 34:15)*

When you take the field against your enemies ... *(Deuteronomy 20:1)*

SOME TRADITIONS do not approve of war under any circumstances. For example, Quakers, as a matter of conscience, do not fight in any wars, even if attacked. On the other end of the spectrum, ancient Roman religions valorized warriors as heroes. Furthermore, the language of "holy war" has appeared a number of times throughout the course of history and is used by some religious proponents today.

As the opening quotations from the Bible indicate, Judaism lies somewhere in between these stances. On the one hand, Judaism certainly does not see war as an ideal state. As a result, every major prayer in Jewish liturgy—including the *Amidah*, said three times daily, the *Kaddish*, said multiple times daily, and the *Birkat ha-Mazon*, grace after meals—ends with a prayer for peace.

And yet, the Torah spells out some rules for war, and the Bible depicts many wars, some of which were commanded by God. Furthermore, the Babylonian Talmud demands that we defend ourselves: "If someone comes to kill you, rise up early in the morning and kill him first" (Sanh. 72a). In addition, it delineates the standards and procedures for determining whether several kinds of wars are justified, and both the Torah and the Talmud define criteria for acceptable military conduct in war.

Historically, however, Jews have not had a lot of experience in making decisions about which wars to wage. This is because Jews have ruled themselves only three times in Jewish history: in the period from the conquest of the Land of Israel to the fall of the First Jewish Commonwealth (approximately 12<sup>th</sup> century B.C.E. to 586 B.C.E.); during the Maccabean period (165 B.C.E. to 63 B.C.E.); and in the modern State of Israel (1948 to present). As a result, the guidelines that come from the Talmud and later Jewish legal literature may not be relevant to modern military conditions. This is for two reasons: first, these guidelines were often created in the absence of real military experience; second, modern military technology transforms the nature of war—at least in degree, if not in kind.

Thus, in order to gain insight from the Jewish tradition on issues regarding war, we need to consider not only traditional sources, but also the values that have shaped the Jewish tradition's views on war and the Jewish tradition in general. Israelis' attempts to consider traditional sources and values in the course of defending their country on a daily basis prove illuminating to the discussion in this volume, especially because these attempts to follow the guidance of traditional Jewish sources on war are grounded in contemporary military realities. The experiences of Jews living outside of Israel also prove instructive as they take part in their own nations' debates over proper rationales for going to war and acceptable wartime conduct.

Some of the questions that have arisen since the earliest human conflicts began are the same as those we face now. They include:

- Is it ever proper to attack someone else? If so, what are cogent justifications for doing so? If not, what should you do if someone attacks you?
- Does it make a difference if you are seeking not to kill, but only to disarm or injure the other person to remove him or her as a threat? How would you apply that analysis to nations at war?
- What should happen to the spoils of war? Why?
- What should happen to prisoners of war? Why?
- Are the justifications and rules of conduct for defense and attack the same for nations as they are for individuals? If not, what are the differences?

Contemporary factors, however, have changed the ways that war is waged in the modern world, raising new questions:

- Given the authority of the United Nations and the World Court to adjudicate disputes, must one try these avenues of resolving conflict before going to war?
- Do the catastrophic implications of the potential use of nuclear and biological weapons undermine all justifications for war?
- New technologies such as stealth bombers, drones, and long-range missiles make it easier to kill people at a distance. What are the moral implications of these developments?

# Introduction

- The technology of modern communications can help to avert war by allowing people to convey their intentions clearly and instantaneously, but it can also aid people in waging war more effectively. How does this raise the stakes for both peace and war?
- The effectiveness of terrorism in our time is, in part, due to coverage in the international media because it spreads fear of further attacks. How should the media cover such attacks in order to spread information and encourage vigilance, while minimizing panic?
- Even people with few financial resources can, with modern technology, create lethal weapons to be used in terrorist attacks. How does this alter the playing field of war and the measures nations need to take to protect their citizens?

The cases and essays in this book seek to address some of these questions.

To what degree do you think your responses to these questions are the same as they might have been had you lived thousands of years ago, and to what degree do you think they are shaped by the world you live in today? How do the issues and questions posed here contribute to your understanding of the morality of war and the methods of waging it in our time?

The Prussian general Carl von Clausewitz once said, "War is nothing but the continuation of state policy by other means." His understanding of war as an alternative to diplomacy not only creates a theoretical construct; it also requires each nation to take diplomacy seriously so as to avoid war whenever possible. It further requires nations to conduct war in a way that will enhance future prospects for peace. Thus, the ethics of war should affect each nation's policy decisions and military tactics. Ideally, this ethical sensibility should also inform your own attitudes and actions when you go to the voting booth or decide to engage in other kinds of political advocacy.

The Jewish tradition ultimately declares each of us personally responsible for communal and national decisions that affect all of our lives. War, by its very nature, involves killing people, which the Jewish tradition prohibits except under extreme circumstances. Judaism demands that, if necessary, we must set aside almost all other commandments in order to save people's lives.

So, as you think about justifications for war and appropriate conduct during war, remember the rabbinic interpretation of the biblical statement that we should "seek peace and pursue it" (Ps. 34:15): the Jerusalem Talmud tells us, "The Law does not order you to run after or pursue the other commandments, but only to fulfill them on the appropriate occasion. But peace you must seek for your own place and pursue it even to another place as well" (Pe'ah 1:1 [4a]). In other words, even as we debate whether, or in what situations, waging war might be morally acceptable, we must always pursue peace in any way that we can.

# Case 1

✤

# National Security

Case 1: National Security

## Case Study

THE ATTACK on the United States on September 11, 2001 starkly raised the question of what responses to terrorist attacks are appropriate, both domestically and internationally.

Domestically, these might include:
- Restrictions on free speech
- Restrictions on assembly
- Monitoring the telephone calls and emails of: non-citizens in America; citizens with known ties to the enemy; citizens suspected of ties to the enemy; any American citizen
- Extensive use of video surveillance in public places
- Monitoring citizens' and/or non-citizens' financial activities through bank account and credit card activity
- Racial profiling
- Increasing surveillance at airports through invasive security machines and/or profiled screening
- Allowing citizens from countries classified as harboring terrorists to enter the country, but only with significant visa and financial restrictions
- Prohibiting entry for citizens from countries classified as harboring terrorists
- Moving suspected terrorists into internment camps

Are any of the above appropriate means of responding to, and seeking to prevent, terrorist attacks on domestic soil?

Do any of the responses above become acceptable if:
- There is an isolated terrorist attack in your country in which many people are killed?
- There are continuous terrorist attacks carried out with the professed goal of destroying your country?
- An enemy has a clearly stated objective to take over not only your country but many others?

- A government is engaging in genocide in its own territory and is liable to do the same in your country if it succeeded in an invasion?

What, if anything, should be done about citizens of your own country who come from the same ethnic or religious background as your enemy?

How do these questions look from the perspective of an American? How do they look from the perspective of an Israeli?

## Traditional Sources

*Compiled by Uzi Weingarten and the Editors*

### On the Duty to Be Loyal to the Government

**1. Joshua 1:16–18**

They answered Joshua, "We will do everything you have commanded us and we will go wherever you send us. We will obey you just as we obeyed Moses ... Any man who flouts your commands and does not obey every order you give him shall be put to death. Only be strong and resolute!"

**2. 1 Kings 2:36–37**

Solomon's instructions to Shimei (who had severely disrespected his father, King David; cf. 2 Samuel 16:5–8):

Then the king summoned Shimei and said to him, "Build yourself a house in Jerusalem and stay there—do not ever go out from there (i.e., Jerusalem) anywhere else. On the very day that you go out and cross the Wadi Kidron, you can be sure that you will die; your blood shall be on your own head."

**3. Mishnah, *Avot* (Ethics of the Fathers) 3:2**

Rabbi Hananiah, The Deputy High Priest, taught: Pray for the welfare of the government, for if people did not fear it, they would swallow each other alive.

### On Privacy

**4. Leviticus 19:16**

Do not go about as a talebearer among your countrymen. Do not stand upon the blood of your fellow; I am the LORD.

**5. Deuteronomy 24:10–11**

When you make a loan of any sort to your countryman, you must not enter his house to seize his pledge. You must remain outside, while the man to whom you made the loan brings the pledge out to you.

**6. Babylonian Talmud, *Pesahim* 112a (cf. *Niddah* 16b)**

Our Rabbis taught: Seven things did Rabbi Akiba charge his son, Rabbi Joshua: My son ... Do not enter your own house suddenly, and all the more your neighbor's house ... Rashi on this passage: "Do not enter your house suddenly," but rather call out to them [those inside] before you enter in case they are engaged in something private. Rabbi Yohanan, when he would go to visit [Rabbi Haninah] would knock at the door, as it says, "its voice should be heard when he comes into the sanctuary" (Exodus 28:35).

### 7. Babylonian Talmud, *Derekh Eretz Rabbah* 5:2

A man should never enter his fellow's house suddenly. All can learn such good manners from the All-Present, who stood at the entrance of the Garden [of Eden] and called to Adam [to announce His presence], "And the Lord God called to the man and said to him, 'Where are you?'" (Genesis 3:9).

### 8. Maimonides (Rambam), *Mishneh Torah*, Laws of Neighbors 2:14, 5:6 (based on Mishnah, *Bava Batra* 3:7 and Babylonian Talmud, *Bava Batra* 60a)

2:14: In a shared courtyard that is large enough to be divided [that is, where there are at least four cubits (six feet) square in the shared courtyard for each family that lives in the houses surrounding the courtyard] or where the owners divided the courtyard voluntarily even though there is not enough to require division, each of the owners can force the others to build a wall in the middle so that one will not see the other when using his part of the courtyard, for injury caused by seeing [another in a private setting] is [legally] injury (*she-hezek re'iyah hezek hu*) ...

5:6: If one of the partners [in a courtyard surrounded by houses] wanted to create a window in his house to the courtyard, another partner can prevent him from doing so because he could see him through it; and if he created it [not knowing the law], he must seal it up. Similarly, partners in a courtyard may not create a door to their house opposite the door of another house or a window opposite another window. But people may create a door to public property opposite another door or a window opposite another window because either can say, "I am like anyone in the public domain who can see you."

### 9. Decree of Rabbenu Gershom (c. 960–1028, Germany) in Louis Finkelstein, *Jewish Self-Government in the Middle Ages* (New York: Jewish Theological Seminary of America, 1924), 31, 171ff, 178, 189

One may not read another's letters.

### 10. Norman Lamm, *Faith and Doubt: Studies in Traditional Jewish Thought* (New York: Ktav, 1971), 295

It should be added that while the discussion in the Talmud concerns visual access to a neighbor's domain, the principle may be expanded to cover eavesdropping as well. One prominent medieval commentator, Rabbi Menahem Meiri (*Beit Ha-Behirah* to *Bava Batra* [ed., Sofer], 6), decides that while we must guard against *hezek re'iyah*, visual surveillance, we need not worry about *hezek shemiyah*, aural surveillance. Hence the wall the partners can demand of each other must be solid enough to prevent over*looking* each other's affairs, but need not be so strong that it prevents over*hearing* each other's conversations. But the reason Meiri gives is not that eavesdropping is any less heinous than spying as an invasion of privacy, but that people normally speak softly when they think they will be overheard. Where this reason does not apply, such as in wiretapping or electronic "bugging," then obviously *hezek shemiyah* is as serious a violation and a damage as *hezek re'iyah*. All forms of surveillance—natural, mechanical, and electronic, visual and aural—are included in the Halakhah's strictures on *hezek re'iyah*.

## On Free Speech and Its Limits
### 11. Midrash, *Leviticus Rabbah* 33:1

Rabbi Shimon ben Gamliel said to his servant Tabbai: "Go to the market and buy me good food." He went out and brought back a tongue. He told him, "Go out and bring me bad food from the market." He went out and brought him a tongue. He then asked him: "Why is it that when I said 'good food' you brought me a tongue, and when I said 'bad food' you also brought me a tongue?" He replied: "It is the source of good and evil. When it is good, it cannot be surpassed; when it is evil, then there is nothing worse."

### 12. Babylonian Talmud, *Eruvin* 13b

Rabbi Abba stated in the name of Samuel: For three years there was a dispute between the School of Shammai and the School of Hillel, the former asserting, "The law is in agreement with our views," and the latter contending, "The law is in agreement with our view." Then a Heavenly Voice announced, "The utterances of both are the words of the living God, but the law is in agreement with the rulings of the School of Hillel."

Since, however, "both are the words of the living God," why was the School of Hillel entitled to have law fixed in agreement with their rulings? Because they were kindly and modest, they studied their own rulings and those of the School of Shammai, and they were even so humble as to mention the opinions of the School of Shammai before theirs.

**13. Midrash, *Numbers Rabbah* 14:4**

Lest a man should say, "Since some scholars declare a thing impure and others declare it pure, some pronounce a thing to be forbidden and others pronounce it to be permitted, some disqualify an object while others uphold its fitness, how can I study Torah under such circumstances?" Scripture states, "They are given from one shepherd" (Ecclesiastes 12:11): One God has given them, one leader [Moses] has uttered them at the command of the Lord of all creation, blessed be He, as it says, "And God spoke *all* these words" (Exodus 20:1). You, then, should, on your part, make your ear like a grain receiver and acquire a heart that can understand the words of the scholars who declare a thing impure as well as those who declare it pure, the words of those who declare a thing forbidden as well as those who pronounce it permitted, and the words of those who disqualify an object as well as those who uphold its fitness. Although one scholar offers his view and another offers his, the words of both are all derived from what Moses, the shepherd, received from the One Lord of the Universe.

# Contemporary Sources

*Compiled by Steven Edelman-Blank*

**On the Duty to Be Loyal to the Government**
**1. Henry David Thoreau, "On Civil Disobedience," Part 2, Section 9 (1849). Available at http://thoreau.eserver.org/civil2.html**

Under a government which imprisons any unjustly, the true place for a just man is also a prison. The proper place today, the only place which Massachusetts has provided for her freer and less desponding spirits, is in her prisons, to be put out and locked out of the State by her own act, as they have already put themselves out by their principles. It is there that the fugitive slave, and the

Mexican prisoner on parole, and the Indian come to plead the wrongs of his race, should find them; on that separate, but more free and honorable ground, where the State places those who are not *with* her, but *against* her—the only house in a slave State in which a free man can abide with honor. If any think that their influence would be lost there, and their voices no longer afflict the ear of the State, that they would not be as an enemy within its walls, they do not know by how much truth is stronger than error, nor how much more eloquently and effectively he can combat injustice who has experienced a little in his own person. Cast your whole vote, not a strip of paper merely, but your whole influence. A minority is powerless while it conforms to the majority; it is not even a minority then; but it is irresistible when it clogs by its whole weight. If the alternative is to keep all just men in prison, or give up war and slavery, the State will not hesitate which to choose. If a thousand men were not to pay their tax-bills this year, that would not be a violent and bloody measure, as it would be to pay them, and enable the State to commit violence and shed innocent blood. This is, in fact, the definition of a peaceable revolution, if any such is possible ... But even suppose blood should flow. Is there not a sort of blood shed when the conscience is wounded? Through this wound a man's real manhood and immortality flow out, and he bleeds to an everlasting death. I see this blood flowing now.

2. **Louis D. Brandeis, "The Jewish Task," an address delivered to the association of Reform rabbis in 1915; reprinted in** *Readings in Modern Jewish History*, **Eliezer L. Ehrmann, ed. (New York: KTAV, 1977), 463–464**

Let no man imagine that Zionism is inconsistent with Patriotism. Multiple loyalties are objectionable only if they are inconsistent. A man is a better citizen of the United States for being also a loyal citizen of his state, and of his city; for being loyal to his family, and to his profession or trade; for being loyal to his college or his lodge ...

There is no inconsistency between loyalty to America and loyalty to Jewry. The Jewish spirit, the product of our religion and experiences, is essentially modern and essentially American. Not since the destruction of the Temple have the Jews in spirit and in ideals been so fully in harmony with the noblest aspirations of the country in which they lived ...

Indeed, loyalty to America demands rather that each American Jew become a Zionist. For only through the ennobling effect of its strivings can we develop the best that is in us and give to this country the full benefit of our great inheritance. The Jewish spirit, so long preserved, the character developed by so many centuries of sacrifice, should be preserved and developed further, so that in America as elsewhere the sons of the race may in the future live lives and do deeds worthy of their ancestors … A conflict between American interests or ambitions and Jewish aims is not conceivable. Our loyalty to America can never be questioned.

## On Privacy and Civil Liberties

3. **Norman Lamm, "The Right of Privacy" in *Judaism and Human Rights*, Milton R. Konvitz, ed. (New York: W.W. Norton & Company, Inc., 1972), The B'nai B'rith Jewish Heritage Classics, David Patterson and Lily Edelman, series eds., 233**

    … the right to privacy is not absolute; for instance, such rights would automatically be suspended where there exists a grave threat to national security. But privacy is more than a legal right; there is also a moral duty for man to protect his own privacy.

4. **Elliot N. Dorff, *Love Your Neighbor and Yourself: A Jewish Approach to Modern Personal Ethics* (Philadelphia: The Jewish Publication Society, 2003), 35–38**

    *The right to privacy is at the core of human dignity.* The more our privacy is invaded, the more we lose two central components of our dignity—namely, our individuality and the respect we command from others. When our innermost selves become the subject for the knowledge and criticism of others, the resulting social pressure will quickly wear away our individuality …

    The community does have a right and, indeed, a duty to establish and enforce some norms, but if the community can know and scrutinize absolutely every one of our thoughts and actions, we will inevitably displease the majority in some ways and lose their esteem in the process. Conversely, the very requirement to honor and protect a person's privacy both stems from, and engenders, an inherent regard for that person. Thus by preserving human individuality and honor, privacy contributes to human dignity.

*Privacy is at the heart of mutual trust and friendship.* If you reveal things I tell you in confidence, I will think twice before trusting you as a business partner, a colleague, or a friend.

*Privacy also enables creativity to flourish,* for it protects nonconformist people from interference by others. Along the same lines, privacy is a prerequisite for a free and tolerant society, for each person has secrets that concern weaknesses that we dare not reveal to a competitive world, dreams that others may ridicule, past deeds that bear no relevance to present conduct, or desires that a judgmental and hypocritical public may condemn.

These moral concerns justify the protection of privacy in any society, but a religious tradition like Judaism adds yet other rationales for safeguarding an individual's privacy. First ... the Jewish tradition teaches us that when we reveal a person's secrets we not only defame that person, but we also dishonor the image of God within that person and thus God Himself.

Moreover, God intends that the Israelites be "a kingdom of priests and a holy people" (Exodus 19:6). Among other things that the Torah requires of Jews so that they might become a holy people ... [is that they] protect a person's home, reputation, and communication by forbidding both *intrusion* and *disclosure* ...

5. **Alan M. Dershowitz, *Is There a Right to Remain Silent: Coercive Interrogation and the Fifth Amendment After 9/11* (Oxford: Oxford University Press, 2008), Inalienable Rights Series, Geoffrey R. Stone, series ed., 174**

Those whose job it is to gather information—by means of interrogation, electric intercepts, spying, and other low- and high-tech mechanisms—may have little or no interest in the admissibility of that information at subsequent criminal trials. Their interest is in real-time *actionable* information that can be used to prevent *future* crimes, especially terroristic ones ...

Pursuant to the Supreme Court's holding and reasoning in *Martinez*, the privilege against self-incrimination now has nothing to say about coercive interrogation, even that which entails tortuous methods, so long as its fruits are not introduced into evidence at the criminal trial of the coerced person. The privilege, as interpreted by the Court, gives a green light to all preventive intelligence interrogation methods. The due process clause may impose some constraints on the most extreme forms of coercion, but even that is uncertain, especially in the context of preventing mass-casualty terrorist attacks.

The hole in our constitutional law is gray, if not black, when it comes to such interrogation. This is not as it should be in a nation that prides itself on the rule of law, especially constitutional law.

**6. Benjamin Netanyahu, *Fighting Terrorism: How Democracies Can Defeat Domestic and International Terrorists* (New York: Noonday Press, 1995), 42–43**

The idea of an absolute civil liberty—whether a "leftist" liberty such as absolute free speech or a "rightist" liberty such as the absolute right to bear arms—should be tempered by political realities, and the attempt to apply it in its pristine form has grave consequences. When a society tries to grant such pockets of unlimited freedom, it provides the proverbial 99 percent of normal citizens with supposed "rights" that they neither want nor need—the "right" to call for the murder of what they deem an obnoxious author, or the "right" to own a grenade launcher. But there are always those in the other 1 percent who, if granted such freedoms, *are* capable of coming up with ways to abuse them. In fact, it is just such supposed rights that are needed to transform a handful of odious but essentially impotent lunatics at the edges of society into a seething menace capable of turning that society into a shambles. Advocates of absolute civil liberties forget that legally protected freedoms are not *ends* in and of themselves; they are *means* to ensuring the health and well-being of the citizens. The United States Constitution, said Justice Robert Jackson, is not a suicide pact. And when a protected "right" in practice results in the encouragement and breeding of terrorist monstrosities ready to devour other members of society, then it is clear that such a right has ceased to serve its true end and must be either revised or reduced.

**7. Irving Greenberg, "The Ethics of Jewish Power" in *Beyond Occupation*, Marc H. Ellis and Rosemary Radford Ruether, eds. (Boston: Beacon Press, 1990), 65**

… since Israel is functioning in the real world, its morality must be exercised and judged in that arena. A normal country—let alone one like Israel that is continually threatened—will not survive if it ties its hands with absolute moral strictures and does not adjust to the pressures of power and the threats posed by its enemies. Using this reasoning, the United States Supreme Court ruled that those dedicated to the overthrow of the system are not entitled to all the constitutional guarantees. To rule otherwise would be to turn constitutional rights into a cover for an assault designed to destroy them. Those who insist that Israel must live by absolute morality are similarly perverting morality, turning it into a battering ram for destruction.

## On Domestic Responses to Terrorist Threats
### 8. Bruce Hoffman, *Inside Terrorism* (New York: Columbia University Press, 1998), 203

The proliferation of religious terrorism also raises a number of other disquieting possibilities and consequences, given that members of many of these groups, sects, and cults are what might be described as "amateur" terrorists in contrast to the relatively small number of "professionals" who have dominated terrorism in the past. Previously, terrorism was not just a matter of having the will and motivation to act, but of having the capability to do so—the requisite training, access to weaponry and operational knowledge. These were not necessarily readily available, and were generally acquired through training undertaken in camps known to be run either by other terrorist organizations or in concert with the terrorists' state sponsors. Today, however, information on the means and methods of terrorism can be easily obtained at bookstores, from mail-order publishers, on CD-ROM or even over the Internet.

### 9. Letty Cottin Pogrebin, "How Could a Jew Do That?" in *Best Jewish Writing 2002*, Michael Lerner, ed. (San Francisco, CA: Jossey-Bass 2002), 219

Israel's heartless or sadistic treatment of the "Other" seems to be proliferating. In response, right-wing apologists would probably say, "these people" deserve it, all of them, because every Arab would destroy us if he could. But at this point in history—given Israel's unquestionable military superiority—I believe we should be less worried about external enemies than about the internal existential threat to the very essence and meaning of Judaism and the Jewish State. In short, if we stop acting Jewish, are we still Jews?

**10. Michael Lerner, "Should Scared Jews Become Tough Jews?" in *Best Jewish Writing 2002*, Michael Lerner, ed. (San Francisco, CA: Jossey-Bass 2002), 28**

As the frenzy around anthrax by mail has demonstrated, no amount of bombings of other countries, rooting out particular networks of terrorists, or suspension of civil liberties can succeed in providing protection in a world in which our biological, chemical, and technological sophistication allows people to kill us if they hate us enough to be willing to lose their own lives. The only protection is to build a world where people won't have that desire.

# Responses

## Homeland Security
### Nadav Morag

**The Effects of 9/11 on the Federal Government**

THE TERRORIST attacks on September 11, 2001 have led to an ongoing debate in the United States as to how to cope with what is widely perceived to be an unprecedented threat to the security of the country and its citizens. Whether or not the terrorists of al-Qaeda and their fellow travelers actually pose such an unprecedented threat can be debated. What is indisputable, however, is that the response to those horrific attacks has been profound and far-reaching.

Among other things, 9/11 led to the largest reorganization of the executive branch of the United States government since the creation of the Department of Defense in the wake of the Second World War. This reorganization resulted in the creation of a mammoth new department under the executive branch, the Department of Homeland Security (DHS). The DHS has been working to redefine the relationship between federal, state, and local governments, thus redefining, at least to some degree, the very concept of federalism on which the nation was founded.

The term "Homeland Security" is uniquely American, stemming from geographic and historic realities. For two centuries (except for the border skirmishes of the Mexican-American War, the small-scale battles against Native Americans, the air defense of Pearl Harbor, and peripheral engagements on two of the Aleutian Islands during World War II), the United States enjoyed the luxury of fighting its wars with foreign enemies overseas. This, coupled with the historic inward focus of American society rooted in the country's relative geographic isolation, gradually led to the development of a dualistic worldview in which the domestic and the international were seen as virtually mutually exclusive. In terms of threats to security, this meant that domestic threats (the "home game" in common parlance in the Homeland Security community) were perceived fundamentally as criminal activities directed against individuals rather than the state, whereas international threats (the "away game") were viewed as being matters of "national security" directly affecting the diplomatic and economic standing of the country, threatening the state, even if they impacted individuals.

The dual nature of how threats were perceived also extended, not surprisingly, to the nature of the response to those threats. Those perceived as domestic criminal threats were dealt with through the tools of law enforcement and the criminal justice system. This necessitated viewing such threats as those of individual criminals (even if the criminal acted as part of an organization) that had to be prosecuted, but whose basic rights and civil liberties were guaranteed, as they are to any individual in society. External, or national security, threats were dealt with using the traditional and time-honored instruments of national power: unrestrained intelligence-gathering, military action, and various coordinated economic and trade measures.

The terrorist attacks of 9/11 forced Americans to reassess this paradigm and brought home the realization that while external threats to national security still exist, the threat from what in military parlance is termed "fourth generation warfare" (attacks by non-state actors such as terrorists and guerrillas, often coming from within a society), has breached the divide between the domestic and the international.[1] As a result, measures that were seen as acceptable for the "away game" now have to be considered for the "home game." Such measures are generally viewed as normal activities in a war zone, and are, in many cases, legal under international law. These include but are not limited to:

- Killing enemy combatants engaged in hostile activity (e.g., assassinating terrorists)
- Setting up internment camps and practicing preventive detention
- Placing restrictions on the freedom of speech and freedom of movement of combatants and non-combatants
- Aggressive monitoring and use of surveillance practices and invasive information-gathering techniques

America's Homeland Security strategy, as outlined by President George W. Bush in the October 2007 iteration of the *National Strategy for Homeland Security*, consists of prevention, protection, response, and recovery,

---

1. William S. Lind, "Understanding Fourth Generation Warfare," *Military Review* (Sept.–Oct. 2004), 13–14.

and includes some of the measures mentioned above.[2] Much of the debate over post-9/11 civil liberties is associated with measures under the "prevention" component of that strategy that seek to keep terrorist attacks from occurring.

## Civil Liberties and National Security

In any democratic society, there will always be a tradeoff between liberty and security. Total liberty, in the sense of the absence of legal and/or moral restraints on the individual, is a very dangerous thing that would inevitably result in the strong denying rights to the weak, thus ultimately restricting liberty for most. At the same time, total security is something that cannot be achieved, since creating the kind of oppressive police state necessary to keep everyone in line would invariably produce a "predatory" state characterized by tremendous personal insecurity due to constant fear of the state and its agents. For a democracy such as the United States then, the question becomes: what is the correct balance between liberty and security, given our current definition of liberty and the current perception of threats to our security?

The answer to this question, in my view, comes down to the basic responsibility of the state: to provide, first and foremost, for the safety of its inhabitants. A state that cannot produce security for its inhabitants will also be unable to provide basic rights and liberties to its citizenry. Providing a bit more security in exchange for a bit less liberty is probably the only realistic option for a state, given current threats. This would not be irreversible, and would enable the country to loosen security measures if the threat dissipates.

Most experts, however, consider the current threat from the Jihadist community to be one that will exist for several decades. Consequently, a policy of greater security cannot be tied to a single terrorist event or even to a chain of events and cannot be driven by attacks, but only by the nature of existing threats and the potential for future attacks, particularly those with mass casualties. Similarly, it does not really matter if the terrorist enemy wants to change U.S. policy in the Middle East, replace the Constitution with the Shari'a, or establish a global caliphate. What does

---

2. President George W. Bush, *National Strategy for Homeland Security* (Washington, D.C.: The White House, 2007), 1.

matter is whether or not the Jihadist enemy is willing to kill and maim large numbers of Americans in order to accomplish its objectives.

Many other democracies have accepted the fact that the nature of the threat from terrorism requires strengthening security at the expense of liberty. Countries such as Israel, Britain, France, and Italy, to name some prominent ones, have laws that allow authorities to detain suspects for relatively long periods of time. Some, like Israel, allow for long periods of preventative detention, detaining someone not because they have carried out or assisted in carrying out an attack, but because they are seen as being likely to do so. These countries also have powers to expel dangerous aliens, conduct aggressive intelligence-gathering activities (often with a dedicated domestic intelligence service, something that the United States lacks), and conduct legal proceedings that provide maximum protection for the state (by, for instance, allowing the state to keep evidence from the defense counsel that might expose intelligence organizations' sources and methods).

Israel has effectively employed a whole range of tactics that are, for the most part, deeply harmful to the civil liberties of mostly non-Israeli citizens, such as the Palestinians in the West Bank and Gaza Strip. These include: restrictions on freedom of movement through the use of checkpoints, barriers, curfews, and closures; administrative detention (as mentioned above); and the assassination of key terrorists, usually for operational, not political, reasons. Such tactics have certainly not endeared Israel to Palestinians, and there is evidence that they have actually increased the motivation and desire for revenge through terrorist activities. But they have resulted in a dramatic drop in terrorist attacks inside Israel. Between 2000 and 2005, close to 1,200 Israelis were killed in terrorist attacks (and some 7,000 were injured), while the past several years have seen barely a handful of attacks with few casualties resulting.

The governments of Israel and the other countries mentioned that have tightened security measures may not define or prioritize civil liberties in quite the manner that some Americans might expect, but they are able to use counterterrorism tools in order to increase security and thus save lives. Civil liberties are not and should not be a goal in and of themselves. Those liberties can and should be viewed as rights, but the most fundamental right is the right to security. If maintaining that right requires some degree of infringement on citizens' individual liberties (and a greater degree of infringement on the rights of individuals suspected of links to terrorism), then this is the price that those of us living in a free society must pay.

**Profiling**

However, the need for increasing security doesn't mean that the government should target particular groups in society. While the 9/11 terrorists were all Arabs (primarily Saudis), Jihadist groups exist throughout the Muslim world from Algeria to Iraq to Pakistan to Indonesia, and consequently there is no single ethnic community with a monopoly over Jihadist views. In Britain, for example, the primary Jihadist threat comes from the large Pakistani-British population, while in France it comes from radicalized North Africans, and in Israel it comes from Palestinians. To use the British example, the attackers that carried out the July 7, 2005 attacks on the London Underground and a public transit bus were primarily British Pakistanis (with one Brit of Jamaican descent). A copycat attack three weeks later that was, fortunately, poorly executed, was carried out by East Africans (Somalis, Eritreans, and Ethiopians), a community that the British Security Service (MI5) did not have on its radar screen.[3]

The lesson here, of course, is that Jihadist terrorism does not fit a particular ethnic profile. Jihadist views are constantly making inroads among various ethnic groups through prison radicalization and growing ties to extreme left- (anarchist and anti-globalization) and right-wing (neo-Nazis, skinheads, etc.) groups. In sum, the threat is not ethnically based, and consequently, targeting only specific ethnic groups with intrusive intelligence-gathering, preventive detention, and other measures is not likely to be effective. Furthermore, targeting specific groups is likely to be counterproductive, for it turns these communities against the authorities—which can have very grave and far-reaching consequences.

Effective intelligence-gathering, the primary tool in the fight against terrorism, requires cooperation from the community within which the terrorists, or potential terrorists, operate. The technological eavesdropping feats of electronic intelligence (signals intelligence—SIGINT) are very impressive, but most truly useful information comes from agents

---

3. This was stated by a senior member of the British Security Service (MI5) in a briefing held on March 12, 2008.

recruited from within the community in which the terrorists operate (human intelligence—HUMINT). If that community distrusts the authorities and believes that government officials are hostile toward them, they are not likely to cooperate or to view the terrorists as a particular threat. Consequently, the authorities need to both do everything possible to avoid targeting entire ethnic communities, and also work to create a sense that the authorities and the community are working together to root out terrorism.

In sum, terrorism, which is designed to disrupt the normal day-to-day affairs in any society and cause people to live in fear, is a far greater threat to personal freedoms than the measures taken by credible democratic countries to safeguard their citizens, economy, and way of life. Any supporters of civil liberties who view government security measures as some sort of conspiracy designed to enslave the population would do well to consider what life would be like, and what the quality of personal freedom would likely be without such protection. Yet, overzealous protection of civil liberties could inadvertently provide terrorists free reign to disrupt the normal course of social and economic activities, and thus inadvertently support terrorist objectives of undermining our social and economic stability.

## Responses to Terror and their Consequences: An Interview with Noam Chomsky

Elliot N. Dorff

*This is the transcript of an interview Elliot N. Dorff conducted with Noam Chomsky on August 11, 2009.*

**Elliot Dorff: How do the questions in this case look as an American, and how do they look from the perspective of an Israeli?**

**Noam Chomsky:** There is something rather crucial omitted from all of those questions—namely, the most important kind of response. The most important way to respond to any criminal act, and terrorism is, of course, a criminal act, is to find out what its roots are. You often discover that the roots have to do with grievances that can be addressed.

Now, we have plenty of experience with this, so take IRA terror, which was quite serious. For a long time, the British responded to IRA terror with the techniques that are described in the case study, and also with more terror of their own. Finally, the British started to pay some attention to the grievances that led to the terror—and they were real. They do not justify the terror, but they help to explain it. Once the British began to deal with the grievances, the terror diminished and, in fact, terminated. That's a sensible approach.

In the examples given in the case study, the terror doesn't come from nowhere. So, for example, take 9/11. Every specialist on the subject—whether it's Michael Scheuer, who was head of the CIA pursuit of Osama bin Laden, or academic specialists, or journalists—discusses the reasons behind terrorist attacks and explains what those reasons are. And some of those reasons are things that should be addressed, and if they are addressed, that could diminish and maybe eliminate the terror. But if they are ignored, and the grievances are simply exacerbated, then you have one of two possibilities: either the terror will increase, or else you will have to carry out massacres and slaughter to try to stop the terror. But all of these issues are overlooked in the series of questions attached to this case.

Another thing that is omitted is that the questions are based on a conventional, but very narrow, concept of terrorism. The questions presuppose that terror is something that *they* do to us and don't address what *we* do to them. So for example, take the United States and Cuba. For 50 years, the United States has launched major terrorist wars and brutal and sadistic economic strangulation for reasons we know very well, because the internal records have been made public. Under the Kennedy administration, Robert Kennedy, the President's brother, was assigned the task of bringing "the terrors of the earth" to Cuba—those are the words of his biographer, Arthur Schlesinger, John F. Kennedy's advisor—and they engaged in very serious terrorist attacks. The economic strangulation had a very definite purpose: to punish Cubans because of Cuba's "successful defiance" of U.S. policies going back to the Monroe Doctrine.

In fact, the same is even true of 9/11. In the West, which of course includes Israel, 9/11 refers to September 11, 2001. Just go south of the border, though, to Latin America. There, that is often called "the second 9/11" because there was another one, September 11, 1973. Let us imagine that the terrorist acts of 1973 in Chile had been carried out on September 11, 2001 in the United States. That September 11th was awful enough, but it could have been worse.

Suppose, for example, that al-Qaeda had been backed by a superpower, and it bombed the White House, killed the President, established a military dictatorship, killed 50,000–100,000 people, tortured 700,000, established a major terrorist center that was overthrowing governments and installing neo-Nazi style dictatorships around the world, then carrying out terror around the world, and also brought in a group of economists who practically destroyed the economy, leading to one of the worst economic crises in U.S. history. That would've been a lot worse than 9/11/2001. But what I described *did* happen in Chile on 9/11/1973. The only thing I have changed is per capita equivalents. The U.S. was behind the overthrow of democratically elected President Allende in Chile—in fact, instrumental in it. What do we say about that?

In the case of Israel, it's too obvious to discuss. Israel is in the Occupied Territories, carrying out acts that even Israeli courts concede indirectly are totally illegal, in violation of the Geneva Conventions. Israel is engaged in very harsh repression; it is invading its neighbors. So, for example, in 1982, Israel invaded Lebanon and killed maybe 15,000–20,000 people, explicitly for the reason of preserving Israeli control over the Occupied Territories. There was no provocation from Lebanon or the Palestinians in the preceding year of the cease-fire, despite regular Israeli violations, including serious bombings. So, yes, if Israel wants to deal with terrorism, it should first of all pay attention to some of the reasons for it. And that is also true of the United States.

**ED: If the United States were to try to alleviate some of the grievances that led to 9/11 here, what are those grievances, and how would you want the United States to respond to them?**

**NC:** We know what the grievances are. In fact, we've known about them for 50 years. Let's go back to 1958. In 1958, President Eisenhower asked his staff why there was a campaign of hatred against us in the Arab world—not from the governments, but from the people. That was a pretty striking year, because at that point, Eisenhower had compelled Israel, Britain, and France to withdraw from their invasion of Egypt. Nevertheless, he recognized that there was a campaign of hatred against us. The National Security Council had pointed out that there was a perception in the Arab and Muslim world that the United States supported harsh, brutal dictatorships and blocked democracy and development, doing so because the U.S. wanted to gain control of their resources. The National Security Council then said, even so, that the invasion of Egypt was basically the right policy, so we should continue it.

Then let's come back to 9/11. After 9/11, *The Wall Street Journal*, to its credit, conducted a study, which it published prominently, of selected Muslims who were sometimes called "Moneyed Muslims," wealthy Muslims—lawyers, professionals, directors of multinational corporations, all of whom were very westernized in their point of view and strongly pro-capitalist and pro-globalization. The study asked them, "What are the grievances that led to 9/11?" The Muslim respondents pretty much repeated the perception the National Security Council talked about in 1958. They said the United States supports harsh, brutal dictatorships and prevents development and democracy.

And by 2001, they had other grievances. One of them was the sanctions against Iraq, which aren't talked much about in the West, but which led the two distinguished international diplomats who administered them for the U.N. to resign in protest because they regarded these sanctions as genocidal. That perception exists now and has long existed in the Arab world. The sanctions killed probably hundreds of thousands of people and devastated the society, meanwhile strengthening the tyrant. So that was one grievance. The other was Israel's occupation of Palestinian territories—harsh, brutal, illegal, undermining the possibilities for Palestinian independence of any meaningful kind, and combined with extensive terror and aggression. These are real grievances; they are not irrational or obscure.

There are others. For example, in the case of al-Qaeda, Osama bin Laden was explicit about his grievances. From his point of view, the United States was occupying the holy places in Saudi Arabia, as we had military bases there. Actually, the Pentagon agreed with him. Paul Wolfowitz explained later that we're looking to move the military bases out of Saudi Arabia to other places in the region to undercut the grievances that inspire al-Qaeda. Many in the Arab world see the West as taking their resources, supporting brutal dictatorships, preventing democracy and development, and carrying out aggression.

After 9/11, the Jihadist movement itself was highly critical of al-Qaeda. There were fatwas denouncing 9/11 and so on. Instead of using that opportunity, George W. Bush carried out aggressive actions—mainly, invasions of Afghanistan and Iraq—which basically drove the Jihadist movement back into support of bin Laden. If you carry out actions that are going to exacerbate legitimate grievances, even at a time when you can move to undercut terrorist activities, that is what's going to happen. And unless these facts are faced, the issues that are raised in the case study are going to be marginal.

**ED: So if you were President Bush, after 9/11, what would you have done?**

**NC:** I would have reached out first of all to the general Muslim and Arab populations, which were appalled by 9/11, and even to the leaders of the Jihadist movement, including clerics at Al-Azhar University and others, and said, "Yes, we understand. We appreciate your condemnation of 9/11, and we should work together to undercut the threat that such terrorist acts will be continued. And we will pay attention to some of your grievances."

So, for example, before the invasion of Iraq, in the case of sanctions, we could have said to Iraq that we'll terminate the sanctions, that we understand that they're murderous, in fact, genocidal. We could have said that we'll move to try to allow Iraqis to settle their own problems as they probably would have done if it hadn't been for the sanctions, and, instead of invading Afghanistan, we could have requested from the Taliban that they extradite people who we suspected of involvement in 9/11. That would have been a very sensible proposal, and in fact, it might have worked.

Case 1: Responses

The Taliban responded to our original requests for extradition by saying they would think about it, if we gave them some evidence. And of course, nobody extradites anyone without evidence.

Instead, the Bush administration simply dismissed them with contempt and basically said, "You don't have any right to ask for evidence from us. We'll bomb you." Remember that the bombing of Afghanistan was not undertaken to overthrow the Taliban; that was an afterthought weeks later. The bombing was undertaken because the Afghans refused to extradite Osama bin Laden without evidence. Actually, we know now why the Bush administration refused to produce evidence: they didn't have it. Without evidence, you will never get cooperation on an extradition request, no matter who the state is. So, therefore, we bombed. And the bombing was bitterly condemned by leading Afghan anti-Taliban activists because it was killing innocent Afghan civilians and it was furthermore undercutting their efforts to overthrow the Taliban from within, they charged.

Then, of course, there is the invasion of Iraq. Once the invasion of Iraq took place, there was overwhelming opposition to it all over the world—Europe, too—and certainly in the Arab and Muslim worlds.

**ED: So the fundamental point that you are making is that you should respond to terrorism by responding to the grievances that cause it.**

**NC:** Not only that. Terrorism is a criminal act, so you respond to it as you do to other criminal acts: you try to find out who is responsible and apprehend them. Since it's an international matter, you can usually get international cooperation in identifying and catching the perpetrators. So you apprehend them, you bring them to justice, and give them a fair trial, just as you do with other criminal culprits.

**ED: Understood. Let us go on to the part of the case that deals with Israel. A large part of the issue is Israel's occupation of the West Bank since 1967. But Israel has withdrawn from Gaza, and nevertheless there were bombs that fell on S'derot daily over the last several years. So what do you think Israel's response to that should have been?**

**NC:** First of all, Israel did not withdraw from Gaza. Gaza is still occupied territory. Israel maintains total control over it. And Israel barely stopped for a day carrying out violent acts in Gaza. As soon as there was an election in Palestine in January 2006, a couple of months after the so-called withdrawal, the election came out the wrong way. It was a free election, everyone agrees with that, but it came out the way the United States and Israel did not want. So instantly, the U.S. and Israel, with Europe tagging behind, began to punish the population severely for voting the wrong way, and that picked up even more in June 2006 and became worse later. So Israel never left Gaza, and it is continuing to punish it. The siege is vicious.

Now, let's turn to your specific question: Suppose Israel was interested in stopping the rockets from attacking S'derot. It should first try peaceful means to resolve the issue. They exist, but Israel does not want to try them.

There could be a narrow effort and a broader one. The narrow effort would be to accept a ceasefire. Israel has never accepted a ceasefire. There were some partial ceasefires, but Israel maintained the siege and then violated ceasefire agreements directly. The most important instance of this was in 2008. Right before the Israeli invasion, there was a ceasefire. It was observed completely by Hamas. The Israeli government concedes that there was not a single Hamas rocket fired during the ceasefire. Israel nevertheless maintained the siege, and in November 2008, Israel just invaded Gaza outright and killed half a dozen Hamas activists. After that, rockets started. Even so, right up until the invasion in December, Hamas kept proposing reinstituting a ceasefire. Israel rejected that. When you reject peaceful means, you have no justification whatsoever for using force—that's elementary. That is the narrow answer.

There is also a broader answer. Israel could stop its criminal activities in the West Bank, which is recognized as being unified with Gaza. As long as it does not do that, it can expect that there will be a terrorist response.

**ED: So if you were an Israeli, my guess is that you would be working to try to resolve some of these political issues—but in the interim, what modes of self-defense would be appropriate?**

**NC:** A ceasefire. A ceasefire is a fine mode of self-defense. The one time when Israel partially accepted it, only partially, it in fact ended the rocket fire.

**ED: And what about the fact that Hamas says outright that it wants the obliteration of the State of Israel?**

**NC:** Look, have you read the Likud charter or the Likud program? Just take their 1999 platform. It says straight out, there cannot be any Palestinian autonomy in the Land of Israel. Now, what is the Land of Israel? It stretches at least from the Jordan River to the Mediterranean Sea. And if you go back further in Likud ideology, it includes Transjordan, too—today's Kingdom of Jordan. That is their policy. Does anybody say, therefore, that we can't deal with the government of Israel? That is what they say in words; we want to know what their policies are.

Israel may not like to hear this, but the policies of Hamas are very close to the international consensus that the U.S. and Israel reject. Namely, they have repeatedly called for a two-state settlement on the international border ... They are not going to recognize Israel as a Jewish state, but the United States does not recognize Pakistan or Iran as Islamic states. It recognizes them, but not as Islamic states. These are all negotiable issues, if anyone were interested in peace. If, in an independent Palestine, Hamas happens to be the dominant political party, it would probably agree to recognize the State of Israel, but focusing attention on that speculation is hardly more than a device to evade the crucial current issues.

**ED: What measures do you think that it is fair for a government—any government—to implement as day-to-day policy for maintaining security and for making sure that terrorists are not able to act?**

**NC:** A government should begin by implementing control of its own terrorists; that is elementary. But take a look at what the settlers do in the West Bank—there's plenty of terrorism. Israel could begin by ending the occupation. Internal to Israel, as long as it is going to carry out actions that are likely to inspire terrorism, it makes sense to take protective measures. So, for example, I do not object to going through security at airports. As long as the government acts to increase the threat of terrorism, then yes, it is going to have to take measures to defend people from it.

**ED: Aside from what goes on at airports, would you permit things like wiretapping and checking of people's monetary accounts?**

**NC:** Wiretapping can be done under court orders. Now, what about checking monetary accounts? The U.S. Treasury Department has a bureau, the Office of Financial Assets Control (OFAC), which has the responsibility to investigate suspicious transfers of funds internationally, like terrorist financing. What does OFAC do? It carries out intensive inquiry into transfers of funds that might violate illegal U.S. sanctions on Cuba.

In fact, it had six times as many people working on that in 2004 as it did on terrorist financing.

Still, one of OFAC's greatest achievements was to close down an Islamic charity, Al-Barakaat, which it claimed was sponsoring terrorism. That got a lot of acclaim in the press, a real victory for the Bush administration. It was later conceded quietly that it was a mistake; they were not financing terrorism. But meanwhile, something else happened. Al-Barakaat was one of the main funders for Somalian civil society. Somalia is a society living on the brink, and a large part of its economy was supported by this charity. When it was closed down, it was a disaster for Somalia.

**ED: So that was, as you say, a mistake. It was a bad mistake …**

**NC:** Let's do something about it, not just quietly say, "Oh, sorry boys, we made a mistake." Let's try to do something about the havoc we caused.

**ED: Is the very methodology acceptable, though, even if it was used badly in that case?**

**NC:** It was not used badly there. It was used *well*. It was used well to promote actual policies, but the actual policies are not undercutting terror. That's a low priority. So, for example, when people in the United States can make tax-free contributions to Israeli terror in the Occupied Territories, *that* should be stopped.

**ED: So the underlying theme here has been that the way that you counter terrorism is by countering the causes of it.**

**NC:** That's the beginning.

**ED: Right.**

**NC:** And if you carry that out, terrorism will be seriously mitigated and maybe ended, as happened in Northern Ireland. But that's only half of it. The other half is that you stop your own terrorism …

**ED: So as not to cause future terrorist acts.**

**NC:** No, no. Because it's wrong. It is just as criminal when *we* do it as when *they* do it. Reagan's terrorist wars in Central America were a far greater crime than anything al-Qaeda has carried out. Israel's invasion of Lebanon in '82 was a far greater crime than anything attributed to Hamas or Islamic Jihad. It's not just that terrorism will inspire more terrorism; it's that it's criminal.

There's a general point here: if the government acts in a way that does not mitigate the terrorist threat by responding appropriately to its causes, but instead exacerbates it by engaging in terrorism itself, and if it does that systematically and consistently, then there will have to be domestic means to protect people from the consequences of these actions. To be clear, I am not suggesting that these are the only causes of terrorism, but they are the ones under our direct control, and dealing with them can significantly reduce terrorist acts, possibly reducing them to marginal criminality—as has happened in some cases.

## Terrorism—A Viewpoint
Joan Schultz

IRONICALLY, I am beginning my response on the subject of terrorism on Sept. 11, 2008. I am writing while flying on a Lufthansa flight from Munich bound for Denver, where I will get on yet another plane to San Diego. Paul, my husband, noted our date of return when we sat with our travel agent, so I have thought about the irony of flying on this date a number of times in the last few days. But I'm not the only one—thousands of others are doing it, too. After going through the airport security designed to keep us safe, security that I never dreamed would ever be required, I have to wonder if someone determined to bring a plane down could still get through with ease.

**Security Measures**
There have been a number of societal changes that have taken place since September 11, 2001. Among them is the awareness of being "politically correct." While standing in line to board a plane, do you look at your fellow passengers? Did you fearfully survey the line prior to 9/11? The average man who appears to be Middle Eastern is now scrutinized by Transportation Security Administration (TSA) representatives. Is that prejudicial? Should the Middle Easterner be questioned more than any other traveler? Should there be a difference between how he and other passengers are treated?

Israeli airport personnel single out certain passengers. They watch, question, and keep watching those they think might be suspicious. Shouldn't TSA personnel across America be trained to do the same? I frequently wonder about TSA personnel's capacity and desire to do their job in an effective, non-abusive manner. Yet, they must do so, following the Israeli model, so that suspicious people may be pulled aside, but treated with basic respect.

In order to be able to protect all people in our country, across all ethnic groups, we must become less "politically correct." Will our freedoms change or be challenged by following the necessary precautions? I do not think so. In fact, our society will be better protected and, thus, our freedoms will be more secure. Some freedoms must be restricted in order to protect greater freedoms.

It is critical that our society change to favor more surveillance than we presently have in place in order to protect us from those who want to do us harm. We should use wiretaps and profiling, but only when those carrying out such practices have been trained to recognize danger and protect our citizenry. The Anti-Defamation League (ADL) has a security program to help law enforcement officers identify risks. For instance, Morris Casuto, director of the San Diego ADL office, is responsible for training law enforcement officers throughout the country to find and aid victims of hate crimes and to recognize people who constitute a security concern.

We must remember that terrorist attacks in the United States, as we have seen in recent years in places such as Oklahoma City, New York, and the Pentagon, have devastating results. There is no monetary value that can be put on a human life, nor should there be on taking the necessary measures to protect life. America is predicted to suffer another terrorist attack in the future. In lieu of saying, "We should have … ," training security personnel properly now might avoid repeating the horrors of 9/11.

**Immigration Policies**

One question that needs to be seriously addressed is whether or not the United States should admit citizens from countries recognized as terrorist safe havens. Only a small percentage of people from such countries are themselves terrorists. It has been said that all Muslims are not terrorists, but all terrorists are Muslims. This is not true, however, as the Oklahoma City bombing by Timothy McVeigh demonstrated. Still, if a country's leaders have stated a goal to persecute or kill those who have different religious beliefs ("infidels"), both in their country and in other nations, or to destroy other countries altogether, the citizens of that country should not gain admission into the United States.

Recently, our government changed its policy and removed the visa requirements for many people coming from foreign countries. Before this change, immigrants seemed to flow easily through immigration in some airports, while in others, agents were far more stringent. Just as TSA personnel need to be better screened for employment and trained uniformly, so do immigration agents. The poem by Jewish poet Emma Lazarus, "The New Colossus," found on the base of the Statue of Liberty, still applies: "Give me your tired, your poor, your huddled masses yearning to breathe free." At the same time, America has changed, as has the rest of the world.

To protect ourselves, visa restrictions must be implemented and uniformly enforced at our airports and at our borders to the north and south. Loosely applied rules, or a lack of rules, can allow people who are threats to enter the country and do us harm.

If a naturalized citizen was born in a Muslim country, how and where that citizen and his or her parents were educated becomes a concern. In certain madrasahs (Islamic religious schools) throughout the Muslim world, young students are taught to hate "infidels." In such schools, inaccurate translations of the Koran spew hatred for non-Muslims. Even young children's coloring books depict violence and promote hatred of Israel. What children are taught when they are young will remain with them throughout their adult lives. Consequently, those from countries known to educate their children in these types of schools who seek citizenship should be routinely and carefully observed during the years that they have a green card, and perhaps after they attain citizenship as well. To prevent future 9/11-type attacks, we must become less liberal and more vigilant about our immigration and citizenship requirements.

**The Model of Israel**

Israel's vigilant posture should be adopted. Any rational person realizes that Israeli society is under siege. Adopting Israeli security measures in an intelligent way, with forbearance and consistency, will help Americans prevent future attacks.

In certain respects, we have already followed Israel's lead. There is a wall between California and Mexico meant to deter illegal immigration and drug trafficking, just as the wall between Israel and the West Bank has cut down on suicide bombings. Some of our airports have X-ray machines similar to those used in Israel to view the contents of checked luggage.

We have started down an extremely long path. Our country is much larger than Israel, making the task of protecting it seem daunting, but the fear of another attack from outside or from within should be motivation enough to continue and enhance our efforts to preserve our safety.

The American perspective on terrorism cannot be compared with the thoughts and constant fears of Israelis. They are surrounded by a hostile Muslim world, and that requires constant vigilance. On the other hand, we have a much larger country to protect, and so we should learn from the Israelis. Our lawmakers should enact their security measures, in ways appropriate to the American context. Yes, that will make government more invasive than it was before 9/11, but terrorist attacks since then in London, Madrid, Bali, Mumbai, and other places demonstrate that we must adopt stronger security measures, if we want to stay alive and safe.

## The Necessity for Strong National Security
### Larry Greenfield

THE AMERICAN Jewish political conversation has broadened in recent years, with younger Jews, Israeli-Americans, Russian and Persian Jews, entrepreneurs and small business owners, Orthodox Jews, post-9/11 "national security" moms and dads, and many pro-Israel U.S. citizens leaning more to the right on foreign policy issues.

The 2008 national elections reaffirmed that the majority of non-Orthodox, urban, and aging Jews continue to focus mostly on domestic policy, remaining rooted in traditional liberal mores and ideology. Yet, even many of these Jews have raised concerned eyebrows over FDR's reluctance to save Jewish war refugees and his failure to bomb the tracks to the Auschwitz death camp during World War II, Jimmy Carter's long-standing and continuing antipathy to Israel, and, more recently, the growing anti-war and anti-Israel rhetoric in many left-leaning academic, church, and media circles. Even more troubling to Jews today are rising Arab anti-Semitism (in mosques, media, and madrasahs), Iranian nuclear proliferation and genocidal threats against Israel, Palestinian suicide terrorism and Jihadist pedagogy in schools and camps, and Hamas and Hezbollah launching rockets and missiles at Israel from Sunni Muslim-controlled Northern Gaza and Shia Muslim-controlled Southern Lebanon.

Americans and Israelis have repeatedly had to learn hard truths about the consequences of appeasement policies in Europe, the human tragedies resulting from a lack of American resolve or from the withdrawal from armed conflict (Vietnam, Afghanistan, Somalia), and the repercussions of naïve and unsuccessful negotiations with insincere actors (Hitler, Khrushchev, Arafat, Ahmadinejad, Kim Jong-il). It appears clear that Israel's unilateral withdrawals from Lebanon (2000) and Gaza (2005), and former Prime Minister Ehud Olmert's proposed retreat from the West Bank (2006) only inflamed the appetites of Israel's enemies. Israeli policy decisions not to respond militarily to Saddam Hussein's Scud missile attacks in the 1991 Gulf War, to repeatedly release jailed Arab terrorists (a discredited tactic, especially since the Victims of Arab Terror organization has established that many released terrorists murder again), and to conclude the war with Hezbollah without victory in the summer of 2006, have all left Israel more vulnerable to future assault.

Weakness is provocative, and human evil smells out opportunities to punish the irresolute. The 20th century alone proved that only victory—not compromise or even containment—could defeat the threats of Japanese imperialism, Nazism, and Communism. The 21st-century battle for peace and security will depend on Western will to defeat Muslim attempts at holy war. It will also depend on American leadership in preventing attacks on democracies, while building moral and strategic alliances for global human rights, prosperity, security, and liberty through engaging in both military action and a war of ideas.

### Balancing Personal Liberties and National Security

Jewish Americans would be wise to consider that throughout American history, leaders and citizens have been mindful of the ever-present balance that must be struck between personal liberties and national security. American law and political culture have generally advocated for individual freedom and limited government. At the same time, however, our nation has thrived because we have also adopted a consistently strong national defense posture.

During crises, such as the Revolutionary period, the Civil War, and World War II, American leadership moved toward the security end of the spectrum between personal liberties and national security and our courts reviewed and approved (and only occasionally rejected) executive branch efforts to restrict personal freedoms in the name of national security. Civil liberties were then often restored and expanded after the national crisis ended.

Today, both conservatives and liberals generally agree with the principles of freedom, limited government, and strong security. Increasingly, however, ideas for how to control the lives of average Americans—through speech codes, taxes, and nanny-state regulation of the workplace and home (guidelines for diets, use of thermostats and plastic bags, types of light bulbs, etc.)—regularly originate from the left side of the political aisle.

Since September 11, 2001, two striking truths have emerged. First, the American political establishment has properly resisted any emotional impulse to restrict the rights of Muslim citizens to free speech, assembly, lobbying, access to courts, voting rights, or political and religious expression, even though we have been engaged in wars in Iraq and Afghanistan against Muslim terrorists. In the years since the worst attack ever on American soil, perpetrated by al-Qaeda-sponsored Sunni

Jihadist men, Muslim citizens have successfully run for office, worked with government officials on intelligence issues, and celebrated their unhindered First Amendment rights to promote sometimes severely unpopular political views about U.S. foreign policy toward the Middle East. The lessons of the controversial internment of Japanese Americans during the 1940s appear to have been well-learned.

However, our libertarian path may leave us vulnerable to sleeper cells and nefarious actors plotting within our country. With this in mind, there have been strong calls to investigate illicit fundraising in some Muslim communities, and security experts have taken measures to prevent Islamist extremists from entering the country. Many mosques in the United States display literature that promotes Sharia Law, implying advocacy of a non-Constitutional regime that could violate our pluralistic democracy. An example of this is the current Sharia courts in Britain that often deny women rights in family disputes. Despite these and other legitimate concerns, however, principles of non-discrimination, due process, and basic fair play remain strong in the United States in the 21$^{st}$ century.

Second, the global war on terror has exposed an ideological divide among Americans and unleashed loathing and paranoia within the political left. This is reflected in a utopian belief in peace that is at odds with the kind of measurable, if gradual, progress made through military campaigns. Frequently, post-modern belief also opposes U.S. strength in international relations and the long-standing concept of American exceptionalism (the belief in the unique role of the United States, as the world's strongest democracy, to lead global affairs). Thus, some intellectuals and urban pundits have revealed hostility toward our honorable volunteer armed forces and their mission.

Even Princeton Ph.D., military strategist, and patriot General David Petraeus was mocked as "General Betray Us" by far-left political organization Moveon.org, which accused him of presenting misleading information on the war in Iraq, striking a new low in the politics of personal destruction. American politicians have sunk to new lows as well. Senator Richard Durbin stated that our troops are like Nazis, Stalinists, and the Khmer Rouge, and Congressman John Murtha falsely charged U.S. troops with committing massacres at Haditha in Iraq.

Although the American military properly responded with revulsion to the abuse of prisoners at Abu Ghraib, prosecuting the offending soldiers and heightening measures to prevent any more such incidents, the American left exploded in misplaced moral outrage. They used the instances of unseemly and unprofessional treatment of prisoners in war zones to castigate the twin goals of liberating Iraq from a mass murderer and brutal anti-Semite, and of attempting to set in motion democratization and modernity in the heart of the Middle East. The left has used a similar campaign to attempt to discredit the entire American defense establishment on the issue of torture, even though the United States stands formally against torture, as demonstrated by Department of Defense policy and adherence to international conventions.

Here again, the left seeks perfection without context and without compassion for Americans working in dangerous environments. There have been rare instances of U.S. military interrogations employing controversial techniques to elicit timely information. The American officials who used waterboarding on Khalid Sheikh Mohammed (the mastermind of 9/11 and the beheader of this writer's boyhood pal Daniel Pearl), reported that Mohammed responded by revealing real-time intelligence about plots threatening New York public landmarks and citizens. In my opinion, waterboarding is too light a punishment for Mohammed; but it should be noted that rough interrogation is not used to punish at all, but instead to discover threats against the U.S. Israel and other allies have also used strong measures in ticking time bomb cases, where lives are hanging in the balance, which even noted civil libertarian Alan Dershowitz has supported with thoughtful approval.

Furthermore, for all the worry about library records and private phone conversations, have Americans actually seen any loss of personal liberty in their daily lives in the name of increased security since 9/11? Apart from some questionable inconveniences at the airport (Do we really need to confiscate Grandma's denture cream?), the answer is no.

Legitimate legal questions have been raised about terrorist surveillance, interrogation, and financial tracking. The courts have ruled both for and against particular procedures and policies. Our political system of checks and balances has also worked to generate creative solutions for treatment of enemy combatants, such as the Guantanamo Bay detention camp. It should be noted that battlefield terrorists held at Guantanamo Bay under U.S. authority eat three square meals a day, exercise, read, write, and pray as they wish.

We are a nation at once dedicated to our Bill of Rights, and also to the common defense. But we now suffer from political correctness and purposeful naïveté about the challenges people must confront on behalf of freedom and public safety.

We need to continue seeking a legal-moral-technological balance to neutralize depraved terrorists' use of cell phones and satellite technologies, the Internet, proxy warriors, non-uniformed surrogates, and even manipulated children and mentally-disabled human bomb carriers. Agents, from the United States Treasury to local law enforcement, work long hours every day to keep Americans safe. They are our neighbors, family, and friends. We owe them honor and gratitude, not fearfulness or name-calling.

Notably, those who were the first to criticize the U.S. government for failing to prevent 9/11 (or, more specifically, for failing to take out Osama bin Laden in Afghanistan in the 1990s) are now often the first to lobby against preemptive military action, strong human intelligence capability, or a forceful foreign policy to detect and deter our enemies. The decline in effective U.S. human intelligence-gathering in foreign countries dates back to the funding cuts associated with the Church Committee reforms of the liberal 1970s Congress.

Today, we also need stronger border security. Again, the American left has been resistant to funding fences and modern technological measures to secure American borders, including monitoring and preventing entry by illegal aliens (some of whom, like the 9/11 hijackers, may be from unfriendly nations). We need to identify and battle against gangs and drug smugglers at our borders and stop sanctuary cities from protecting such bad actors who then engage in criminal activity inside our country.

We also need stronger national security, and a stronger advocacy and diplomacy on behalf of U.S. interests and ideals, than that which we can achieve through participation in international organizations. As the United Nations fails to prevent genocide or human rights abuses, as U.N. soldiers sent as peacekeepers bully civilians, as corrupt U.N. officials reward tyranny, and as abusive bullying and demonizing of Israel runs rife in the U.N. and in Muslim countries, we must consider a new path. Perhaps a Liberty Alliance that would reward countries with aid and trade in exchange for promoting human rights, economic growth policies, non-proliferation of weapons of mass destruction, and friendly alliance with the United States, could provide a workable model for an effective international organization.

## The Lessons of Jewish History

Jewish views on war and peace have always been rooted in the ethics of serving and preserving human life. Normative Judaism has always abhorred both pacifism and unjustified warfare. It has sought peace through strength and realism, promoting both the beating of swords into plowshares (Isa. 2:4), as well as the beating of plowshares into swords (Joel 3:10). Overcoming a persecuted Jewish past, the modern Jewish State of Israel is the result of both ancient dreams and the nightmare of Jewish impotence and passivity.

At times, great dangers require new measures, technologies, and approaches be used to protect human life. The only successful answer to Nazism was its destruction by the armed forces of the United States and our allies. Fortunately, our nation moved past isolationism and anti-war philosophies to unite for victory. The most direct existential answer to longstanding European hatred of Jews was the founding of Israel. In 2003, 70 years after Hitler took power, Israeli Air Force pilots performing in an air show over Auschwitz hummed "*Hatikvah*" ("The Hope"), Israel's national anthem, as they headed back to Israeli headquarters. Self-defense wears a uniform.

Jewish Americans, sobered by the historical realities of Jews' encounters with global affairs, are now more evenly balanced on the political spectrum, at least with regard to foreign policy and the need for security. This is appropriate, for Jewish history informs us that we should seek to respect both legitimate authority and ordered liberty, always secured by noble defenders at home and abroad.

## Politics, Rights, and Security
Ben Murane

WITHIN THE Jewish community there is already a fiery debate over the extent to which Israeli security should trump Palestinian human rights. On the spectrum of curtailing rights, from increasing surveillance to subjecting groups to wholesale internment, I rank the military occupation of the Palestinian territories uncomfortably closer to the latter. I come to this judgment after spending time with Israeli human rights experts, both on the ground in the West Bank and through my career as an Israel educator in the Jewish communal field. I do not come to this judgment lightly, and I rely on those in the Israeli human rights field to help put my personal experiences in context.

I first approached the issue of the military occupation as most American Jews do: from afar. From a distance, the idea of checkpoints, a security barrier, and martial law may seem perfectly reasonable. To combat terrorists intent on killing masses of civilians, harsh measures such as targeted assassinations, home demolitions, the restriction of goods and traffic, random home searches, property seizure, and night arrests can sound necessary. Yet it seems that terrorism in Israel has often been an excuse for the *carte blanche* violation of rights.

But describing these measures as necessary curtailments of rights for the sake of security is not only simplistic, it is downright disingenuous. We cannot ignore that many Israeli security measures are flawed because they are implemented by politicians intent on keeping some or all of the territories as a political concession to hard-line constituents, or as a tool to pressure Palestinian leaders to adopt a compromise suitable to Israel's interests. We cannot discuss Israel's security needs without mentioning the very real threat of terrorism; but we also cannot discuss those needs unless we explain how and why security measures are implemented.

My point is twofold: First, it is misleading to use the Israeli-Palestinian conflict as an example of a circumstance in which sacrificing certain rights for greater security is justifiable. Second, any proposal to sacrifice rights for security should consider the lessons learned from the Israeli-Palestinian conflict, the main one being that rights and security are especially in conflict if a political objective interferes. I will present two cases that prove these assertions and demonstrate the complex issues involved with Israeli security.

### Case 1: Hawara Checkpoint

Imagine that you are a 19-year-old Israeli soldier staffing a checkpoint in the West Bank. You are one of four soldiers dealing with a hundred Palestinians standing in line, and are responsible for carrying out your orders, which are murky, but involve conducting random searches to discern wanted and suspicious individuals. It's a hot day, people are irritable, you have already worked three hours, and you are going to be there for another five.

Today, the line of Palestinians is rowdy, they are angry, and are pushing closer and closer. You exhort them to back up, wait patiently, and have their IDs ready. They are not obeying, and the safety of your friends and your mission are at risk.

You know that in the past, soldiers have been stabbed or shot at checkpoints like this. If you become lenient, the crowd will start taking liberties with your orders and will not maintain proper distance from you. There is also the possibility that if you do not check persons as ordered, an act of terror will occur. But if you are too tough in carrying out your orders, you might increase hostilities. What do you do?

### Response: You Cannot Have a Moral Occupation

There are no easy answers to the case of the Hawara checkpoint. The claim made by the Israeli veterans group Breaking the Silence, that Israeli soldiers manning checkpoints often commit acts of violence, is ugly and uncomfortable. But Breaking the Silence has documented cases upon cases that demonstrate the difficult decisions soldiers assigned to checkpoints make to protect lives and carry out their assigned missions.

In 2005, the Israel Defense Forces (IDF) Educational Corps videotaped the Hawara checkpoint in order to develop a training video and promote to a critical world how humane the Forces are. Their interviews with young soldiers who described the kind of violent treatment necessary to maintain order were haunting and damning. Soldiers were taped taking rowdy and stiff-necked individuals out of line, out of sight of their families, beating them, and then returning them to the line. The young soldiers explained to the cameras with chilling honesty the necessity of asserting dominance in such instances. The Educational Corps footage was promptly buried.

One of the videographers leaked the footage to the Israeli press, causing a public uproar. Two of the Hawara soldiers were court marshaled and punished. However, 56 members of their unit wrote a joint letter to the IDF Chief of Staff demanding that the punishment be revoked. The offenses were standard procedures, they argued, and were carried out upon the instructions of their commanders. Since they each had committed the same offenses, if anyone was to be jailed, then they should all be jailed. The two soldiers were being used as scapegoats in an impossibly unfair situation.

Breaking the Silence, the veterans group that had been insisting that soldiers engaged in violent behavior at checkpoints, was vindicated when, in December 2007, the Israeli military released a study saying that 25% of Israeli soldiers stationed at checkpoints had participated in "severe abuse" of Palestinians, as reported in the Jewish Telegraphic Agency.[1] Veterans testified that the percentage of soldiers who commit acts of abuse is likely higher. If abuse is this commonplace, we are led to wonder whether or not checkpoint security measures are terribly misguided.

The veterans who collected testimonials of abuse found that soldiers are caught between three objectives. Yehudah Shaul, co-director of Breaking the Silence, explains:

> You can have only two of the three: a moral army, security, or an occupation ... If you want human rights, you have to give up either the occupation or security. If you want a moral army, you have to give up either the occupation or human rights. If you want the occupation, you have to give up either having a moral army or security. You cannot have all three. You cannot have a moral occupation.

Thus, the question of whether Palestinian rights should bow to Israeli security concerns is complicated by another variable: occupation. Is it necessary for Israel to be in the West Bank in the first place? Can the Israeli army act in a moral fashion when it is enforcing the occupation of Palestinian territory?

**Case 2: Ba Webe Checkpoint**

On September 23, 2004, I waited at a checkpoint between Jerusalem and the West Bank called Ba Webe ("the little door" in Arabic). The

---

1. "Israel Report Finds Widespread Checkpoint Abuse," Jewish Telegraphic Agency, Dec. 16, 2007. Available at http://jta.org/news/article/2007/12/16/105913/israelicheckpoints.

checkpoint was a pile of concrete blocks eight feet high topped with barbed wire, which blocked a side street between houses. A section of the pile had been toppled, and hundreds of people were pouring back and forth over the fallen blocks. The garden walls of the adjoining private yards had also been knocked down, and more adept climbers were scaling over the walls, carefully shimmying through gaps cut in the barbed wire.

Easily a thousand Palestinians crossed the checkpoint every day. Men dusted white powder off their business suits after scaling the walls. Old women handed bags of laundry and fruit over the pile of bricks. Elementary school students avoided cutting their new clothes on the barbed wire. Teenagers flirted with each other while waiting for others to cross. On both sides of the barricade, two noisy taxi stations and impromptu markets bustled with activity.

Sometimes a military Jeep with two Israeli border policemen sat watching from afar. It wasn't there most days, but on the days it was, the policemen sat there, observing, never interfering. A police station had also been established in a confiscated home nearby, and army vehicles came and went with regularity.

The scene was eerie for its discontinuity. Twenty-four hours earlier, a female suicide bomber had detonated an 11-pound belt of explosives in the French Hill neighborhood of Jerusalem, less than a 10-minute car ride away. She was intercepted at a bus stop bound for downtown Jerusalem and detonated herself to prevent capture. Two Israeli policemen—Lance Cpl. Menashe Komemi, 19, and Lance Cpl. Mamoya Tahio, 20—died and 17 bystanders were injured. That year, up to that day, 26 terrorist attacks had killed 83 people and wounded 294 across Israel, according to the Israeli Foreign Ministry's web site.

Thus, I wondered as I sat watching the Thursday morning activity: Why weren't the border police in the Jeep checking anyone? Why did the security wall cut through this part of East Jerusalem—dividing Arabs from Arabs—instead of cutting between the Jewish and Arab neighborhoods? Why was there a two-kilometer-wide gap in a nearby section of the wall?

From August to December, while I lived in Israel, there were nearly 20 terrorist acts in which 42 people died and 187 were injured. Yet, I never once saw a viable security operation at Ba Webe, one of the busiest intersections between Israel and the Occupied Territories. Why?

Jewish Choices, Jewish Voices: WAR AND NATIONAL SECURITY

**Response: What Security?**
The majority of checkpoints I encountered in late 2004 resembled Ba Webe, where security conflicted with political reality. Ba Webe was left open and unpatrolled in all likelihood because of the two-kilometer gap in the security barrier just a few minutes drive away. The Israelis intended to build the wall around the largest settlement, the 40,000-person, self-contained suburb of Ma'ale Adumim, so that it would be on the Israeli side. However, doing so would have effectively cut the West Bank in two, a political act so controversial that Israel has been unable to proceed. Yet to close Ma'ale Adumim outside the wall would risk offending important Israeli constituents. Thus, the wall remains incomplete, with the two-kilometer gap at Ma'ale Adumim, to this day. With such a gaping hole, there has been little reason to seriously enforce the Ba Webe checkpoint.

The politics of the wall only deepen from there: Instead of separating Israeli Jewish neighborhoods from Palestinian neighborhoods, the barrier ostensibly runs along the municipal border of Jerusalem and the West Bank, an Arab urban sprawl of approximately 257,000 people, according to the Israeli Central Bureau of Statistics. Yet, the barrier makes key deviations to include undeveloped land outside the municipal boundaries on the Israeli side and to exclude a dense Palestinian refugee camp that is within municipal boundaries. The effect is to include as much land and as few Arabs as possible.

If the wall were truly intended for security, the route along which it was built would have been drastically different. In 2004, Israeli human rights groups successfully petitioned the Israeli Supreme Court to reroute a segment of wall constructed through the center of an Arab village. Defense experts with the Council of Peace and Security have testified that the wall route was not planned by security officials but by allegedly pro-settlement politicians.[2] One could argue, therefore, that it would not be the Army's fault if the construction of the wall violated human rights, because they built it on orders they received from their superiors, civilian members of government.

However, the suggestion that security measures necessarily reduce individual rights is only part of a wider conversation. If political

---

2. "Summary of the Council's Involvement in Petitions to the High Court of Justice in Matters Concerning the Security Fence," The Council for Peace and Security, May 27, 2007. Available at http://www.peace-security-council.org/articles.asp?id=611.

compromises were made, perhaps a balance between promoting security and protecting rights could be struck. For instance, if Israeli settlements were removed from the West Bank, the need for checkpoints there would be minimal. If the security barrier were rerouted between Jewish and Palestinian neighborhoods, the intrusion on Palestinian life would not be entirely eliminated, but would be significantly reduced. In both cases, Palestinians would regain some freedom of movement, without the safety of Israeli civilians being jeopardized.

**Conclusion: Politics Is the Key**

Most Americans do not have the authority to directly enforce security measures or make decisions that infringe on others' human rights. But we can play a role in creating those measures and making those decisions—when we vote, donate to a cause, endorse a political petition, or express an opinion. As participants in the political process, we must influence that process to prevent the perpetuation of a false dichotomy between rights and security.

Americans do not live next door to a hostile foreign body as Israelis do. Yet, in recent years, sweeping reductions in civil rights have been proposed to improve our security. There are countless examples of this, from the creation of the Guantanamo Bay detention camp to heightened domestic surveillance measures. The Executive Branch rapidly increased its power through legislation like the Patriot Act and the Bush administration's liberal interpretation of presidential authority. It is a shame that the fervor in the wake of 9/11 prevented us from asking relevant questions about the agenda that was behind this expansion of executive authority. We did ourselves a disservice that we only now are seeking to reverse.

It is widely recognized that the security measures imposed by the Bush administration, including, ultimately, the war in Iraq, were unnecessary and served ulterior objectives. Political ideology, not security, was the guiding consideration that led to the implementation of these measures. Thus, it is our responsibility to ensure that a fully honest discourse surrounds security decisions, which are often guided instead by simplistic frameworks that threaten the creation of and participation in acceptable solutions for all sides.

The Jewish community too frequently uses terrorism as an excuse to accept Israeli human rights violations instead of addressing terrorism's political causes. It damages Jews' moral foundation to use the Israeli-Palestinian conflict as a guide in situations where there is a similar choice to be made between protecting people's rights and strengthening security, such as in the battle against terrorism in the U.S. Based on my experience, any proposal to sacrifice rights for security is suspect and should be thoroughly examined.

If the American and Israeli Jewish communities weighed the policies of their governments and expressed their reactions to those policies by participating in the political process, we might just find ourselves closer to achieving security, human rights, and ultimately peace for all.

# Case 2

## Justifications for War

# Case Study

### A. Just War

Since 1941, the United States has engaged in a variety of military conflicts, some of that were clearly justifiable, and some less so. They have included: World War II (1941–45), the Korean War (1950–53), the Vietnam War (early 1960s–1975), the invasion of Grenada (1983), the first Iraq invasion in 1990–1991 (Operation Desert Storm), the Bosnian War (1995), the War in Afghanistan (beginning in 2001), and the second Iraq invasion, which began in 2003.

Since its founding in 1948, Israel has also engaged in a variety of military actions, including: The War of Independence (1948–49), the Suez Canal Crisis (1956), the Six-Day War (1967), the Yom Kippur War (1973), the invasion of Lebanon (1982), responses to the First Intifada (beginning in 1989) and the Second Intifada (beginning in 2000), the second Lebanon invasion (2006), and the invasion of Gaza (2008–2009).

What are the criteria that make a war just? Have they changed in light of modern technological developments in weapons and communications? Given those developments, which, if any, of the following would be just rationales for abandoning diplomacy and engaging in war?

- Your country is being invaded by another country.
- Your country has been subjected to a blockade of all of your points of entry.
- Your country has been subjected to an economic boycott by all surrounding countries.
- Citizens of your country have been taken hostage by another country and threatened with execution.
- Your country has been made a subject colony by another country that will not relinquish control peacefully.
- Some of the population in your territory wants to secede and establish their own country, but the majority does not want to let them.
- Another country in which your country has a vested interest is invaded by a third country.

- Another country in which your country does not have any economic interests or to which your country has no treaty obligations is invaded by a third country that has threatened genocide.
- Your country is aware that another country's government is committing acts of genocide against its own people.

## B. Self-Defense

When the State of Israel was founded, David Ben-Gurion decreed a doctrine of *tohar ha-neshek,* saying that military force may be used only in self-defense. Known as "purity of arms," this principle is encoded in the Israel Defense Forces' code of conduct, which calls for a proportional response to violence and humane behavior in combat. This doctrine raises many questions concerning the justifications for war. For example:

- What is the moral principle behind Ben-Gurion's doctrine?
- What constitutes self-defense?
- What constitutes a proportional response?
- Can offensive or preemptive actions be part of a strategy for self-defense?
- What new developments in weapons technology make this doctrine difficult to follow?
- Is Ben-Gurion's doctrine feasible in today's world?

Case 2: Justfications for War

# Traditional Sources

*Compiled by Uzi Weingarten and the Editors*

## The Centrality of Peace

### 1. Midrash, *Numbers Rabbah* 11:7

Great is peace, for all blessings are contained in it … Great is peace, for God's Name is peace.

### 2. Psalms 34:15

Seek peace and pursue it.

### 3. Jerusalem Talmud, *Pe'ah* 1:1 [4a]

The Law does not order you to run after or pursue the other commandments, but only to fulfill them on the appropriate occasion. But peace you must seek in your own place and pursue it even to another place as well.

### 4. The *Kaddish*

May the One who brings peace to the universe bring peace to us and to all the people Israel. And let us say: Amen.

## The Nature of Peace

### 5. Isaiah 2:3–4

For instruction shall come forth from Zion,
The word of the Lord from Jerusalem.
Thus He will judge among the nations
And arbitrate for the many peoples,
And they shall beat their swords into plowshares
And their spears into pruning hooks:
Nation shall not take up
Sword against nation;
They shall never again know war.

### 6. Micah 4:2–5 (same as Isaiah 2:2–4, and then the following:)

But every man shall sit
Under his grapevine or fig tree
With no one to disturb him.
For it was the Lord of Hosts who spoke.
Though all the peoples walk

Each in the names of its gods,
We will walk
In the name of the Lord our God
Forever and ever.

## Invasion and Preemptive Strikes
### 7. Exodus 22:1–2

If the thief is seized while tunneling [under a wall for housebreaking], and he is beaten to death, there is no bloodguilt in his case. If the sun has risen on him, there is bloodguilt in that case.

### 8. Maimonides (Rambam), *Mishneh Torah*, Laws of the One Who Injures or Damages 1:16

Anyone who injures his fellow intentionally anywhere [that is, whether on public or private property] is liable for the five remedies [for injury—namely, for the injury itself, for time lost from work, for medical expenses, for pain, and for embarrassment]. Even if he entered his fellow's property without permission and the owner injured him, [the owner] is liable, for he [the owner] has the right to eject him [even forcefully] but not the right to injure him. But if the one who entered [without permission] was injured [accidentally] by the owner, the owner is free of liability. If the owner is injured [accidentally] by the intruder, the intruder is liable, for he entered without permission …

### 9. Babylonian Talmud, *Berakhot* 58a, 62b; *Yoma* 85b; *Sanhedrin* 72a

The Torah [thereby] says: If someone comes to kill you, get up early in the morning [or preempt] to kill him first.

### 10. Babylonian Talmud, *Eruvin* 45a

Rav Judah stated in the name of Rav: If foreigners besieged Israelite towns, it is not permitted to sally forth against them or to desecrate the Sabbath in any other way on their account … This, however, applies only where they came for the sake of monetary gain, but if they came with the intention of taking lives, the people are permitted to sally forth against them with their weapons and to desecrate the Sabbath on their account. Where the attack, however, was made on a town that was close to the frontier [the loss of which would constitute a strategic danger to the other parts of the country], even though they did not come with any intention of taking lives but merely to plunder straw and hay, the people are permitted to sally forth against them with their weapons and to desecrate the Sabbath on their account.

## The Nature of War
### 11. Ecclesiastes 3:1–8

A season is set for everything, a time for every experience under heaven …
A time for slaying and a time for healing …
A time for loving and a time for hating;
A time for war and a time for peace.

### 12. Babylonian Talmud, *Sotah* 44b

Rava said: All [i.e., the Rabbis of the majority opinion and Rabbi Judah] agree that the wars waged by Joshua to conquer Canaan [and the war against Amalek] were commanded; they also agree that the wars waged by the House of David for territorial expansion were voluntary; they differ with regard to wars [Israelites undertake] against heathens so that they shall not march against them [that is, preemptory attacks]. One [Rabbi Judah] calls them obligatory and the other [the majority opinion] voluntary, the practical issue being that one who is engaged in the performance of a commandment is exempt from the performance of another commandment.

### 13. Maimonides (Rambam), *Mishneh Torah*, Laws of Wars and Kings, 5:1–2

1. The first war a king wages is a war of mitzvah. Which is a war of mitzvah? The war of the seven nations (i.e., the Canaanite nations who lived in the Land of Israel and whom Israel displaced), and the war of Amalek, and aiding Israel from an enemy who comes at them. Then he [may] wage a permitted war, which is a war with other nations to expand Israel's boundaries …

2. For a war of mitzvah [the king] does not need permission of a court, but wages on his own [authority] at any time, and compels the nation to go [to war] with him. But for a permitted war, he may

take the nation only in accordance with a court of seventy-one [the Sanhedrin].

**14. Benedict de Spinoza, *Theological-Political Treatise*, chap 18, section 5**

If we try to calculate the periods in which the Israelites were allowed to enjoy complete peace, we shall find a significantly vast difference [between the periods without and with kings]. In the time before the kings, they often passed forty and even, on one occasion (you may hardly believe this), eighty years, in concord, without foreign or internal wars. But as soon as the kings took control, the reason for going to war was no longer, as before, peace and liberty but rather glory, and we read that all the kings fought wars except only Solomon, whose virtue, i.e., wisdom, flourished better in peace than in war. Deadly lust for power took over, rendering the path to the throne very bloody for many of them.

# Contemporary Sources

*Compiled by Steven Edelman-Blank*

**The Nature of War**

**1. Reuven Kimelman, "The Ethics of National Power: Government and War from the Sources of Judaism," *Perspectives* [February 1987], 10–11**

The Talmud classifies wars according to their source of legitimation. Biblically mandated wars are termed mandatory (*milhemet mitzvah* or *milhemet hovah*). Wars undertaken at the discretion of the Sanhedrin (or its legal equivalent such as the modern Israeli Knesset) are termed discretionary wars (*milhemet reshut*).

There are three types of mandatory wars: 1) Joshua's war of conquest against the seven Canaanite nations; 2) the war against Amalek; 3) a defensive war against an already launched attack. Discretionary wars are principally composed of expansionary efforts undertaken to enhance the political prestige of the government or to secure economic gains.

The first type of mandatory war retains only historical interest. Having lost their national identity already in ancient times, the Canaanite nations have been removed from current consideration …

The secondary category of mandatory wars, viz., that of the war against Amalek, has been rendered operationally defunct either by comparing them with the Canaanites or by viewing them as the embodiment of sheer evil and postponing the battle to the immediate pre-messianic struggle.

The two remaining categories, defensive wars (which are classified as mandatory) and expansionary wars (which are classified as discretionary) remain intact ... Intermediate wars such as preventive, anticipatory, or preemptive defy so neat a classification. Not only are the classifications debated in the Talmud, but commentators disagree on the categorization of the differing positions in the Talmud.

## 2. Edwin C. Goldberg, *Swords and Plowshares: Jewish Views of War and Peace* (New York: URJ Press, 2006), 17

It is important to emphasize the fact that, according to ancient Rabbinic tradition, direct revelation from God ceased more than two thousand years ago. Henceforth the only means of understanding God's will is to read and interpret the Bible. This vital insight means that no additions to the list of the seven Canaanite nations and the Amalekites will be forthcoming. It is impossible to add any more recent nations to the list, even if over the centuries certain countries have merited such inclusion due to their nefarious treatment of the Jewish people.

## 3. Abraham Joshua Heschel, "The Reasons for My Involvement in the Peace Movement" in *Moral Grandeur and Spiritual Audacity: Essays,* Susannah Heschel, ed. (New York: Farrar, Straus and Giroux, 1996), 225–226

When I concluded in 1965 that waging war in Vietnam was an evil act, I was also convinced that immediate and complete withdrawal from Vietnam would be the wisest act. Realizing the hopelessness that such a proposal would ever be accepted by the then-current administration, I formulated my thought by saying: True, it is very difficult to withdraw from Vietnam today, but it will be even more difficult to withdraw from Vietnam tomorrow. Above all, it was a war that couldn't be morally justified, for war under all circumstances is a supreme atrocity and is justified only when there is a necessity to defend one's own survival. It is politically illogical, I thought, to assume that Communism in

South Vietnam would be a greater threat to the security of the United States than Communism in Hungary or Czechoslovakia.

As much as I abhor many of the principles of Communism, I also abhor Fascism and the use of violence in suppressing those who fight against oppression by greedy or corrupt overlords. In addition, the war in Vietnam by its very nature was a war that could not be waged according to the international law to which America is committed, which protects civilians from being killed by military forces.

**4. Michael Walzer, "War and Peace in the Jewish Tradition" in *The Ethics of War and Peace: Religious and Secular Perspectives*, Terry Nardin, ed. (Princeton, NJ: Princeton University Press, 1996), 95–96**

... a Jewish war was, for almost two thousand years, a mythical beast. There are no examples; none of the rabbis after Akiba (who may have participated in the Bar Kochba revolt) had any experience of warmaking. This is one of the meanings of exile: Jews are the victims, not the agents, of war. And without a state or an army, they are also not the theorists of war ... It is an interesting outcome of the exile that Jewish writers, religious and secular, played an important role in working out the idea of oppression but virtually no part at all in working out the idea of aggression. Their attention was focused on justice and domestic society, where they had an uncertain and subordinate place, not on justice in international society, where they had no place at all.

## Defensive War and Preemptive Strikes

**5. Bradley Shavit Artson, *Love Peace and Pursue Peace: A Jewish Response to War and Nuclear Annihilation* (New York: United Synagogue of America, 1988), 210**

Only one type of warfare, defensive war, is still permitted. Only combat that is responding to an attack, only defense in order to prevent imminent killing can be vindicated morally. All other warfare is ethically unjustifiable. And it is that position which most authorities of *halakhah* have asserted for almost two thousand years. Judaism has established an impressive legal edifice to reflect its ethical opposition to state-organized killing. The very simplicity of the usable law asserts the force of the moral statement—to choose to wage war is unethical.

6. **Elliot N. Dorff,** *To Do the Right and the Good: A Jewish Approach to Modern Social Ethics* **(Philadelphia: Jewish Publication Society, 2002), 173–174**

   These positions [about justifications for a preemptive attack] clearly range over a wide spectrum, but notice that they all justify preemptive wars for defensive purposes only. Revenge is not countenanced as a motive for a preemptive strike, and neither is intervention to secure the rights of people in another nation. The talmudic, medieval, and modern positions that we have been considering until now may vary widely in their assessment of what constitutes a threat to personal and national security, but it is that which is the motive for any preemptive military action. Initiating a war is justified only to save lives, not to punish an enemy nor even to promote the welfare of the citizens of another realm.

   Consequently, it should not be surprising that Jewish law as it has developed in medieval and modern times makes several prudent requirements of those charged with deciding whether to engage in war, especially a preemptive attack. War is permitted only when the anticipation is that the lives preserved by waging a defensive war are likely to be greater in number than those lost through the war itself. The medicine must not cause more harm than the illness. Similarly, war is permitted only when there is sound military reason to assume that Israel will be victorious, for otherwise war would be tantamount to suicide, which is forbidden … Even the justification of self-defense must be invoked with reason and military knowledge for it to be a sufficient sanction for war.

7. **Diane Balser, "Plotting the Middle Path to Israeli-Palestinian Peace: The Role of American Jews" in** *Righteous Indignation: A Jewish Call for Justice***, Or N. Rose, Jo Ellen Green Kaiser, and Margie Klein, eds. (Woodstock, VT: Jewish Lights Publishing, 2008), 258**

   If nothing else, the 2006 war in Lebanon brought home the fact that military might cannot be the solution to all of Israel's problems. After the bombs cleared in Beirut, Israel was still at risk from Hezbollah, and the country itself was divided on whether the war was necessary or effective. Simply put, discussion about the efficacy of the Lebanon war or Israel's reliance on military force in general would require a paradigm shift of frightening proportions. For years, pride in Israel's ability to defend itself served to ease the pain of our losses over centuries of Diaspora, and soothed fears raised by ongoing anti-Semitism. How do we understand an Israel for which straightforward military victory is no longer a foregone conclusion? So much of the Israel national narrative is rooted in the notion of the powerful Jewish warrior; while some in Israel have clearly become comfortable with questioning that part of the narrative, perhaps the Diaspora continues to hold on to that narrative too tightly.

# Responses

## War in the Jewish Tradition
Michael Walzer

THE JUDGMENTS that we make about American wars, and also about Israeli wars, are shaped by both contemporary moral doctrines and international law. They are generally not shaped by the central texts of the Jewish tradition—the Bible, the Talmud, and medieval codes (Maimonides' *Mishneh Torah* chief among them). When I wrote my book *Just and Unjust Wars*, I read the Jewish sources, but my arguments were directly influenced by Catholic just war theory. In fact, my book is a secularized version of that theory. Why are the Jewish sources less useful than one might think they would be?

The Zionist answer to this question is the best one. Arguments about politics, and especially about war, are carried on in sovereign states whose political leaders have to make decisions about whether, when, where, and how to fight, and whose citizens have the opportunity to support or criticize those decisions. But for almost 2000 years, from the time of Bar Kokhba to the time of Ben-Gurion, Jews didn't have a state; no Jewish leaders were making those kinds of decisions. For all those years, the Jews practiced only local politics on issues such as how to manage the *kahal* (community), how to pay for the synagogue, how to raise money for welfare services, and so on. We had no "high" politics, no politics of war and peace. And it is only high politics that generates theories about when it is right (and wrong) to fight against others. Statelessness is a condition of deprivation, and one of the things it deprived Jews of was a full-scale political theory.

In biblical times, of course, Jews had a state, and so the Bible provides some material out of which a Jewish political theory and moral code for war could be constructed. The problem is that this often isn't material we can feel comfortable about. Consider, for example, the question of genocide. I strongly believe that it is right to go to war to stop mass murder in someone else's country—as we should have, but didn't, in Rwanda in 1994, and as we are unlikely to do in Darfur at the moment I am writing this piece. Jews have special reasons to support the use of force in cases like these. But the reasons come from our experience, not from our tradition.

They do not come from our tradition because the Bible actually includes a commandment, reiterated several times, to exterminate the seven Canaanite nations. Writers working within the tradition have great difficulty with this commandment. It is the word of God, so they cannot deny its rightness, and yet they know in their hearts that it isn't right. Hence, they resort to interpretive maneuvers. They say that the nations of the world have gotten so mixed up that we can't identify the Canaanites anymore. We would kill them if we could but, fortunately, we can't find them. And, as Edwin Goldberg says in his book *Swords and Plowshares*:

> It is important to emphasize the fact that, according to ancient Rabbinic tradition, direct revelation from God ceased more than two thousand years ago … This vital insight means that no additions to the list of the seven Canaanite nations and the Amalekites will be forthcoming. (p. 17)

Thus, no new nations can be added to the list of those we have to kill.

But if we are to oppose genocide *as Jews*, then surely we need to be able to say that the biblical genocides should have been opposed. Or we at least need to say that we now recognize their wrongness, even if that involves arguing with God. But we have precedents for arguing with God. Abraham argued against God's destruction of Sodom and Gomorrah, though he stopped short of a flat-out condemnation of what God was doing. His last question was: "What if ten [innocent ones] should be found there?" (Gen. 18:32) Surely he should have kept going—what if there were five, or even one? And since this was an argument only about adults, Abraham should also have insisted that all the children in the two cities were innocent—like the 120,000 children of Nineveh, "who do not yet know their right hand from their left," for whose sake God spared the city, against the wishes of the prophet Jonah (Jon. 4:11).

We have work to do before we can use biblical texts as the basis for arguments about war. The Rabbis called Joshua's wars to conquer the land and kill the Canaanites "commanded" (*mitzvah*), because they came from God's specific instructions. But we need also to consider the wars of David, which the Rabbis called "optional," "discretionary," or "permitted" (*reshut*). These were wars, as Maimonides says, "to enlarge the borders of Israel and to enhance [the king's] greatness and prestige" (*Mishneh Torah*, Kings 5:1). Yet, are wars of conquest really optional? Contemporary moral theory would say flatly that they are not, and most Jews today would agree with that judgment. It is the people resisting such wars who would be fighting justly—even if they were fighting against King David.

In the Talmud and in the rabbinic commentaries on the Talmud, there are only two kinds of war: commanded and permitted. But these two need the complement of a third kind, namely, prohibited wars. In Israel today, religious scholars are working to develop this third category and to find precedents for it in the old texts. This is important work that would have begun long ago had there been a Jewish state (or two or three Jewish states) whose citizens were arguing about whether and when to fight.

A prohibited war is an unjust war, of which there are many examples. Wars to convert or kill heathens, such as crusades and Jihads, are unjust wars. So are wars of conquest, and wars for plunder and slaves. Genocidal wars are obviously unjust and prohibited, and so are wars fought for the purpose of "ethnic cleansing." The defense of a tyrannical regime against its own rebellious subjects is unjust, as is the defense of empires and colonies against national liberation movements. All of these are also prohibited wars.

The hardest questions arise with regard to preemptive and preventive wars. In the Talmud, in the passage from Tractate *Sotah* 44b, two sages disagree about "an attack to diminish [the military capabilities of] the Gentiles so that they do not bring [an attack] upon them [Israel]." One says that this is a commanded war; the other insists that it is only an optional war. Of these two choices, "optional" seems correct to me. What is being considered here is preventive war: the threat lies in the future, perhaps the distant future, and political leaders and their advisors may disagree about the extent of the threat. How urgent is it to respond with immediate military force? Perhaps it would be enough just to strengthen the army, or fortify the border, or seek new alliances instead of using force. Judgments might reasonably differ about the viability and morality of these possibilities, but if they are real possibilities, we might want to say that engaging in preventive war instead would be prohibited.

The classic test case is the Israeli attack on Egypt in 1967. This wasn't a preventive war, since the Egyptian threat to Israel wasn't distant or speculative. It was immediate, urgent, and concrete. Response to a threat of that sort, where you can see the attack coming, is called "preemptive." Preemption is much easier to justify than prevention, and the case of Israel in June 1967 has convinced many people that, when you are certain that an attack is on its way, attacking first is the right thing to do. I remember well how awful those first days of June were—the terrible fearfulness, even in the Diaspora, where we had nothing to fear for ourselves. But we were afraid for our friends and fellow Jews in Israel. Then, I remember the relief when Israel's preemptive strike was successful. The fearfulness Jews experienced before the Six-Day War justified that war, bringing about wide recognition that no one should have to live under threats of that sort.

But the standard "just war" is a war of self-defense against an actual attack in progress, not an expected attack. Self-defense is always justified, and so is a war to help people who are fighting in self-defense. The era of the Second World War provides many examples of both, and for people of my generation, Jews especially, these are probably the examples that most influenced our ideas about when it is right to fight. The German attack on Poland is an obvious example of aggression, and the Poles' defense of their country, though it was doomed, was nonetheless just. Similarly, Albania and Greece's defense against Italian aggression was just, and so was Finland's defense against Russian attack. The decision of Britain and France to come to the aid of Poland, even though there was little that they could actually do, was certainly just. Two years later, the American decision to join the war against the Nazis was just as well. It would have been even more morally defensible if the U.S. decision had come earlier, not as a response to a German declaration of war, because helping the victims of aggression is inherently good. When aggressors are as murderous as the Nazis were, fighting to stop them is an especially good thing to do.

The war against Nazi Germany was certainly a just war. But was it, according to the old rabbinic categories, a commanded or an optional war? I am inclined to say it was commanded, that is, obligatory. But that isn't the answer given by contemporary international law, which recognizes a right to be neutral, as the U.S. was for the first two years of the Second World War and as Sweden and Switzerland remained for the whole war. Neutrality in the face of Nazism seems morally questionable even if it is legally permitted. But if we insist that all states should join just wars, or at least support them—if not militarily then materially and politically—then we deny the overall moral legitimacy of neutrality. And we also deny the fact that wars can be optional. If just wars are always commanded and unjust wars are always prohibited, then there is no room for the rabbinic idea of optionality.

Optionality is certainly an idea that we need to question and consider. It is not clear that the Rabbis were wrong to identify some wars as "wars of choice," but former Israeli Prime Minister Menachem Begin was sharply criticized by many Israelis for fighting what he called a "war of choice" in Lebanon in 1982. A war that isn't morally necessary requires an excess of justification. If we can choose it, we can also refuse it. I have already suggested that preventive wars may be wars of choice, but speculative and distant dangers don't justify actual wars. Preemption, by contrast, is certainly justified, but it seems to be a chosen act. Yet, we might also think of it as obligatory if we think that political leaders should not wait for their country to be attacked, perhaps fatally, if they can attack first. These are hard questions, and I am not sure that they can be answered in any definitive way. The great advantage of the category of "optional" war is that, by incorporating the element of choice, it forces us to think very carefully about what to do (and what not to do) when faced with real or perceived threats.

Finally, pacifism gets short shrift in the Jewish tradition. Peace is one of the highest values in Judaism, and perhaps because of our statelessness, there is hardly a trace of militarism in Jewish thought. It isn't the warrior but the scholar who is most admired in the tradition. Often in Jewish history, it was the better part of wisdom to surrender rather than fight, as the prophet Jeremiah argued in the face of overwhelming Babylonian power. In the Middle Ages, there were Jewish writers and religious leaders who celebrated martyrdom, and very few who celebrated resistance. But the arguments that I have been working through in this piece demonstrate that, throughout most of our history, Jews have believed that it was sometimes right to go to war.

Most Jews today still believe that, remembering the Second World War or reflecting on the dangers that Israel faces. However, most of us also believe that sometimes war isn't right. Wars can be just or unjust, commanded or prohibited, and sometimes, they can be optional. It is a moral requirement to join the argument about which conflicts fit into which categories. That is why Jewish writers today are engaged in adapting the Jewish tradition to the needs of statehood. We are learning from theorists of just war and from scholars of international law. And, as always, we are learning from our own experience in what is, as it has always been for Jews, a very dangerous world.

## From the Dream of an Ideal Society to the Reality of Self-Defense
Donna Robinson Divine

UPON BEING awarded an honorary degree for his service as Israel's chief of staff during the Six-Day War in 1967, Yitzhak Rabin began his acceptance speech by wondering why The Hebrew University of Jerusalem would bestow an academic prize on a soldier for simply discharging his military duties. "What have those who are professionally occupied with violence to do with spiritual values?" he asked. He then answered his own question by noting the special character of the Israel Defense Forces as "an expression of the Jewish People ..." and by enumerating its "numerous tasks directed to the ends of peace ... [and to] ... strengthening the nation's cultural and moral resources."[1]

The Six-Day War, whose outcome was regarded as Israel's greatest military victory, ironically generated the country's most intractable insecurities and began to dispossess the nation's army of its exceptional status. In addition to remaking the map of the Middle East, the war became the paradigm of a new kind of combat wherein territory strengthened defenses against attacks by traditional armies but weakened them against the forces of terror. The initial euphoria created by the 1967 victory stemmed from the belief that past sacrifices in battles would finally be redeemed in peace treaties with Israel's Arab adversaries. This was dampened, however, systematically and incrementally, as the line between home front and battleground became increasingly blurred. By the time peace treaties were negotiated with Egypt and Jordan in 1979 and 1994 respectively, they neither put an end to the carnage in Israel's streets nor were they expected to do so. The Six-Day War eventually created a deeper awareness in Israel of what military action could achieve. It also eroded the nation's innocence about whether it could maintain its much-vaunted "purity of arms" doctrine (using force only for self-defense) while trying to fulfill the noble Zionist mission of raising up a Jewish state.

The struggle for Jewish independence had once generated ambitions not simply for a state like all other nations, but also for a new kind of social order marked by justice and equality for all. Before Zionists established

---

1. Yitzhak Rabin, "Address by IDF Chief-of-Staff Lieutenant-General Yitzhak Rabin on Acceptance of Honorary Doctorate From Hebrew University Mt. Scopus," June 1967, Israel Ministry of Foreign Affairs. Available at www.mfa.gov.il.

Israel as a sovereign state, their movement was a phenomenon seemingly infused with magnetic force—charged not only with providing persecuted Jews a safe haven or survivors of Nazi genocide a refuge, but also with binding Jews together in a community committed to high moral principles. War had little place in this nation-building worldview except as a tool of defense. Permanent confrontation was unimaginable. But from the beginning of their struggle for statehood, Zionists had to adjust to their utopian ideals' collision with reality.

**The Establishment of the State of Israel**
Israel's very establishment as a sovereign state provides one of the clearest examples both of how Zionist leaders conceived of their responsibilities and of how difficult it was for them to match their actions with their idealistic theories. The messianic vision that gave Zionism its momentum could not bring it its greatest success—the establishment of a state in 1948. That achievement came not from the movement's utopian idealism but rather from its capacity to set priorities, discipline most of its members, and acknowledge that promises of founding a Jewish state on a social order advancing justice and peace, simply could not be kept.

Although the conventional histories of Israel's founding tend to advance the notion that it remade the Jewish nation and formed a new collective identity, Israel was not established simply by a collective act of will. Zionist discourse may have been permeated with utopian urges, but Zionist policies succumbed to reality. While the discourse treated the future as more imperative than either past or present, state-making decisions recognized the need to deal with the political landscape of the moment as it actually was. Thus, above all, the process of creating a state depended on the willingness and capacity to compromise.

Zionists therefore accepted the United Nations' Partition Resolution of 1947 precisely because it granted Jews sovereignty. Statehood, even over a truncated territory, seemed better than any of the other plausible alternatives. It was certainly preferable to the political solution foreshadowed in Great Britain's 1939 White Paper, in which Jews would have to live as a minority in an undivided Palestine.

Zionists understood well the costs of accepting the 1947 U.N. resolution. For some, dividing Palestine meant surrendering the hope of establishing a society consonant with values of justice and bi-national harmony. For others, cutting up Palestine represented a violation of what were taken to be sacred religious imperatives and internationally recognized historic rights. To many Zionists, accepting partition seemed tantamount to a radical repudiation of the very goals that had inspired their most fervent commitments and of the many sacrifices made to build a national home. Finally, many wondered if the proposed geography of a new Jewish state offered sufficient land and resources for the tasks confronting the Jewish people in the aftermath of the devastating impact of the Second World War.

Despite its costs, the U.N. proposal was determined to be acceptable by the Zionist leadership precisely because it offered Palestine's Jews sovereignty. The concept of "sovereignty" has been assigned many, sometimes incompatible meanings over the centuries, but at its core is the notion of autonomy, which in political terms means the capacity to defend oneself and, when necessary, to wage war. Conscious of what it meant to be stateless, Zionist leaders accepted the U.N. partition resolution in 1947, despite deep misgivings about many of its stipulations, because they recognized not only what needed to be done for the Jewish people, but more importantly, what *could* be done.

Notwithstanding international backing that transcended Cold War antagonisms, Israel faced severe tests of its will and its capacity to preserve the U.N.'s grant of sovereignty. The Arab world, rejecting the idea of dividing Palestine, launched attacks aimed at nullifying the Partition Resolution as soon as the U.N. officially adopted it. During those first months of violence, Palestine's Jews fought to preserve the borders of the state as they had been mapped in the partition plan. But casualty figures were high, with the heaviest violence occurring in cities where Jews and Arabs lived side by side. Jewish body counts began to weaken global resolve and support for the idea of partitioning Palestine.

The use of more aggressive tactics by Jewish fighters, starting in March 1948, began to turn the tide of battle by reducing casualties while increasing security and bringing relief, particularly to Jerusalem's Jewish population, which until then had been cut off from its coastal lifeline. From this point onward, the fate of the Jewish state depended less on what was happening at the U.N. and more on the military actions of Jewish forces fighting across Palestine. The borders of the Jewish state that were drawn on the map of the partition agreement were dissolved in battle.

Although Israel won its War of Independence, it still had to demonstrate to its citizens, as well as to its friends and enemies, that it could keep that independence. In the wreckage of war, its borders were under dispute, as they were the outcome of ceasefire agreements, not permanently mapped in treaties of peace. For many Palestinian Arabs, expelled from their homes during the war, those borders were illegitimate, if not meaningless. Not wishing to let their land slip away forever, many crossed back over the borders for that year's harvest. Others, inflamed by nationalist sentiments, refused to accept the loss of Palestine and returned to settle scores. Israeli retaliatory raids stopped terrorists on their way to murder Israeli citizens, but also killed peasants trying to gather crops in the fields they had sown before the outbreak of the war. Israeli military sweeps of villages harboring groups that sent people to infiltrate Israel's borders and attack its citizens, sometimes left women and children among the rubble. Yet, official government pronouncements tended to hide the bellicose actions of Israeli soldiers.

Thus, the War of Independence and subsequent military actions created national heroes, giving young Israeli men and women the opportunity to demonstrate their commitment to their nation by calling them to service, even though they would have to confront dangers far beyond those customarily encountered in an ordered society. And although Israel's founding in 1948 stirred hopeful visions of what a Jewish state could be, it also triggered fear for what the state could be forced to become, given hostile circumstances and the population's tendency for relentless self-scrutiny. For instance, when the wounds of war were made visible in these early years, they typically appeared in literary works, between the hard covers of books, without ever entering the political discourse.

These narratives did not engender moral imperatives, perhaps because the darker aspects of Israel's strategic predicament called for action that conflicted with its ideal of decorum, which had been firmly forged on the principle of stoic survival. Silence and emotional restraint had become values demonstrative of the commitment to national purpose. Until the impact of the 1967 Six-Day War was fully felt, Israelis had an articulated sense of their own distinctiveness, even as the ceasefire lines commanding their emotional attachment could be understood as temporary. Those lines had been drawn by the outcome of war in 1947–1948, not by internationally recognized, more permanent peace agreements.

The experience of its first war in 1948 has weighed heavily on Israeli life, helping to shape the main principles of the country's national security doctrine: minimize casualties even if doing so requires preemptive attacks; bring the fighting to the enemy's territory; and hold all countries from which cross-border strikes are launched accountable for their actions. In the wake of the war, military strategists also argued that the armed services should be allowed a quick and overwhelming application of force not only to destroy the enemy but also to deter it from taking the field again. Additionally, population size served as a consideration in naturalizing these principles and in imagining geographic boundaries. In fact, then, as now, national security views flowed as much from concern about numbers as about territory, even though the demographic issue was then seldom directly engaged.

While several wars tested but did not essentially change the basic components of Israel's security doctrine, the Six-Day War forced a radically new application of that doctrine, as Palestinians brought terror to Israel's cities, roads, and military bases and attempted to wreak havoc upon its civil order. The long-standing notions that the sacrifices of war would bring peace and that battles could be won without compromising or stretching the rules organizing a nation's civil society could no longer remain intact.

**The Current Reality**
When, in 1967, the Israel Defense Forces crushed the strongest of Arab armies, it released the Palestinian national movement from the stifling control of the Arab world. This resulted in a deep and prolonged confrontation with new and increasingly lethal forms of terrorism. The need to counter terrorist attacks led Israel's government to create fortified checkpoints, assassinate high-level terrorist operatives, demolish the homes of terrorists' families, and eventually, establish a set of electronic sensors—the so-called "fence" or "wall"—to deter and help capture infiltrators. Israelis still believe that the more decisively its army overwhelms would-be assailants, the less likely those assailants will be to search for ways to launch attacks.

Even if Israel's enemies have a common language of rage, they still constitute a multitude of forces seemingly fighting for different objectives, who hope that somehow bloodshed will bring forth and define a new order. For Arabs, and particularly for Palestinians, the lack of clarity about objectives has meant that armed struggle has remained paramount, often at the expense of alternative strategies that might have returned a portion of historical Palestine to Arab control.

Israel has thus had to prepare for at least three types of warfare simultaneously: a conventional war against large numbers of soldiers armed with tanks and guns remains a possibility, even though the threat has receded because of the peace treaties Israel has signed with Egypt and Jordan. There is also a risk of war involving weapons of mass destruction delivered by missile strikes or through acts of terror. Finally, the Iranian battle with the United States over regional hegemony in the Middle East has resurrected the armed Palestinian struggle, now led by Hamas and aided by Hezbollah.

While this has not changed the fundamentals of Israel's national security doctrine, it has altered its calculus, partly because now the country must fight simultaneously within and outside its frontiers. Israel has had to find new tactics with which to protect the lives of its citizens even as such measures were essentially conceived within the old framework of minimizing casualties. Missile attacks have diminished Israel's strategic depth because missile batteries have been placed deliberately and provocatively among women and children. These are almost impossible for Israel to destroy without incurring civilian casualties. Thus, while Israelis pursue and seek to obliterate terror networks and to punish and deter the states that harbor them, this has often led to military actions widely condemned as excessive.

Although since 1993, Israel has made efforts to accommodate Palestinian national goals, the failure to achieve an agreement to that end has severely damaged the country's security. To counter terrorist attacks, Israel has reoccupied parts of the West Bank from which it withdrew in the 1990s, when its government took the peace process for granted. It constructed a security fence to block terrorists dispatched to stage attacks in Israel's population centers from getting into the country. This measure improved security for the Israeli citizens, but brought condemnation from many countries and international organizations. Finally, that Iran has helped resurrect and embolden Palestinian militancy because of its own ambitions for regional hegemony has only made it less favorable and more dangerous to move forward toward peace.

Even with Israel's military advantage, the threats against it remain mortal. Thus, Israel has had to prepare its defenses with the gravity of a people who once again face the possibility of destruction. In celebrating over 60 years since its founding, Israel also marks over 60 years of battles that its founders never wanted, but were prepared to accept as the price for realizing a Jewish state.

## The Challenges of Using Self-Defense as a Justification for War: An Interview with Rebecca Vilkomerson

Elliot N. Dorff

*This is the transcript of an interview Elliot N. Dorff conducted with Rebecca Vilkomerson on October 21, 2009.*

**Rebecca Vilkomerson:** I want to start by saying that I'm coming from the perspective of an activist.

**Elliot Dorff: An activist for …**

**RV:** I work for an organization called Jewish Voice for Peace. We're a community of activists inspired by the Jewish tradition that works toward a just peace in Israel and Palestine, based on human rights, equality, and international law.

**ED: From that perspective, what would you say about Ben-Gurion's *tohar ha-neshek* doctrine, that one may take up arms only in defense?**

**RV:** I think it's very interesting to quote David Ben-Gurion about the defense doctrine that war is only just when it's defensive, and I think, generally, I would agree with that. I do believe there are justifications for war.

However, I think that his theory is very different from the current reality. The Israeli army is called the Israel Defense Forces, despite the fact that Israel has actually started the majority of its wars. I'm thinking specifically about the most recent example, the war on Gaza. Israel was the aggressor in that war and used overwhelming firepower against an essentially defenseless population. As a result, a high number of civilians were killed. So I think, despite the fact that there's this doctrine, the reality is often quite different.

**ED: So you're saying you don't think that Israel has actually followed the *tohar ha-neshek* doctrine even though Ben-Gurion announced it?**

**RV:** That's correct.

**ED: What is the moral principle behind Ben-Gurion's doctrine?**

**RV:** I think the moral principle about wars worldwide is that they are only justified when they are defensive. Again, I'm speaking as an American, and also as someone deeply involved in the Israel-Palestine conflict. International law has been formulated over the past half-century in the wake of some of the greatest worldwide conflagrations, and I think that the doctrines behind those laws, such as self-defense, are often theoretical, but are worth trying to follow.

**ED: Why are they worth following?**

**RV:** It's a matter both of self-interest and of morality. First, you don't want to have chaos, with a system of "might makes right," and so there has to be some sort of restraint on military power. What happens in the world shouldn't be based around military power. We need to have respect for countries' borders and for the rights of civilians not to be attacked. I think, then, that there's a difference between getting civilians involved and getting soldiers involved. International law regulates the rules of war between soldiers and between armed forces, and protects civilians to ensure that they are not involved.

**ED: So your analysis of Ben-Gurion's doctrine is that it is important, both for pragmatic and for moral reasons, to avoid anarchy and to respect the rights of civilians within a country. How do developments in weaponry make his doctrine hard to sustain?**

**RV:** I actually think that the new developments in weapons—I assume we're talking about nuclear weapons—actually very much reinforce these principles. I suppose you could make the argument that different countries possessing these weapons keep attacks from happening, but I would say that because these weapons exist and their use can be so much more devastating than the use of weapons on a more individual or less indiscriminate level, it's even more important to be very measured and very cautious in deciding to wage war.

**ED: Yet, when Ben-Gurion was talking about the *tohar ha-neshek* doctrine, he was referring to the use of "light arms"—that is, a gun that you would hold yourself in facing one other person.**

**RV:** I think there is a certain level of individuality on the battlefield when humans meet humans, where you realize that what you're doing is not just pushing a button. When you can just push a button and kill thousands of people, it becomes too easy.

On the other hand, I wouldn't want to romanticize hand-to-hand combat. I think that it's cruel and terrible, and certainly there are many, many accounts from people who have fought that way about how terrible it is. So I'm not sure that, as a doctrine, the fact that you're an individual holding a weapon, making an individual decision, necessarily makes using a weapon any better. You can certainly behave very badly in that circumstance, too.

**ED: So then, the doctrine says that you should go to war only for the purpose of self-defense, but you've already raised some of the issues of defining what constitutes defense. Is stockpiling weapons, for example, including nuclear weapons, a mode of defense? Some people think that the reason why there hasn't been a nuclear war is because both the former Soviet Union and the United States had so many nuclear weapons that it would result in instant annihilation of both countries and possibly the whole world if either one of them started a war. So the argument has been that having a large stockpile of nuclear weapons actually acts as a defense mechanism.**

**RV:** This is one of those arguments that works until it doesn't. In the grand scheme of things, we've had a nuclear world for 50 or 60 years, and we've been extremely lucky so far that nuclear war has been avoided. But that doesn't mean that it will be avoided in the future, and if it's not, that would be so incredibly devastating. I'm in favor of nuclear disarmament, and ultimately a nuclear-free world, simply because of the potential for disaster if that doesn't happen, and because, generally speaking, I don't really trust the ability of governments to always make wise decisions.

**ED: And then, of course, you also have the problem of non-governmental actors getting a hold of some of these weapons.**

**RV:** That's correct, and that's an enormous risk. But I think that the more these weapons are out there in the world, the more likely that is to happen.

**ED: Can offensive and preemptive action be part of a strategy for defense? During the Six-Day War, after then Egyptian President Nasr had closed the Straits of Tiran and engaged in all kinds of bellicose verbiage, together with Syria and Jordan, the Israelis bombed all of the Egyptian planes on the ground on the first day, before the Egyptians actually started military action, as a preemptive act. Do you think that was justified as an act of defense?**

**RV:** What I think is that that kind of justification is very tenuous. I certainly wouldn't want to say that it's never justified to make a preemptive strike of that kind. I think, in theory, an attack on military planes on the ground is a pretty legitimate response to keep a devastating war from happening.

However, my criticism about that reasoning is that, too often, what is called defense is actually offense. For example, in the most recent Gaza war, I do not think that the Hamas rockets coming from Gaza toward Israel were enough of a threat for Israel to launch the attack that it did, even though I think the rocket launches were illegal and wrong. And I think, especially in recent years, that Israel has used its overwhelming military strength in an extremely negative and damaging way.

And I would say the same about the second Lebanon War, that the incident that ignited the war was certainly wrong, but that Israel's response was way more than defensive. It was, in fact, aggressive, and involved occupying another land and using firepower to destroy not only civilian lives, but civilian infrastructure.

I think it's too easy to say that an action is defensive or preemptive. You can almost always find some reasoning that justifies being aggressive, and so that's my concern with it.

**ED: In the early 1980s, Israel bombed Iraq's nuclear reactor. Do you think that that was justified?**

**RV:** Well, it's impossible to say if that was justified because we don't actually know what was there and what Iraq would have done with it. You could certainly say that it was incredibly hypocritical for Israel to decide that, while it was capable of handling nuclear weapons, Iraq was incapable of handling them, despite the fact that Israel has never acknowledged having nuclear weapons and has refused to be part of the family of nations that has regulated its nuclear weaponry.

Certainly, Israel has proven itself to be quite aggressive militarily, and yet it still also maintains nuclear capabilities. Yet, if the position were reversed and one of the Arab countries had come and bombed Israel, bombed Dimonah, where Israel's nuclear facilities are, you can imagine what kind of reaction that would've caused. So I think that that bombing was hypocritical at best.

**ED: Okay, so can you generalize as to what you think the criteria are that make a war just?**

**RV:** I think, generally, if a population is in danger, if a legitimate government is in danger, then a war to protect it is just. Furthermore, I think there's a difference between justification for a war and then the actual conduct of that war; I think those are two separate issues. You can have a just war that's unjustly conducted, and I would certainly argue that the United States was very much justly involved in World War II, but I disagree with using nuclear weapons in Hiroshima and Nagasaki. I think that was unjust conduct. So I think those are two separate issues.

**ED: What if your country has been subjected to a blockade of all of your points of entry?**

**RV:** A very, very small country that has no way to, for example, feed itself, if it's blockaded—think of Iraq, which suffered under very harsh sanctions in the lead-up to the two Iraq wars—is different from the United States, for example, which if it is blockaded, has self-sufficiency and could take care of itself regardless. I think generally you could say it *could* be justification for war if your country is blockaded.

**ED: Okay, so that leads to the next question: Your country has been subjected to an economic boycott by all surrounding countries. Is that a reason to go to war?**

**RV:** This is an interesting case where I think things have changed, given the global economy. You can have a country that's economically blockaded by all the surrounding countries, but yet is still doing perfectly well because it's trading with a country across the world or it's using some other way of global communication and exchange. So I think, for me, that that circumstance would not rise to the level of a justification for war. But justification needs to be determined on a case-by-case basis.

**ED: What if citizens of your country have been taken hostage by another country and threatened with execution?**

**RV:** No, I don't think that is a justification for war.

**ED: So what would you do?**

**RV:** I think there are tons of examples. Recently, I read about an American reporter who was held hostage for seven months in Afghanistan, and no military action was taken. To enter a war in response to such a situation is a very serious step to take, and so I think you really need to first of all, go through all the other options. And second of all, if those options fail, you need to evaluate—unfortunately—whether one person's life is worth putting two societies in conflict with one another.

**ED: If your country has been taken over by another country that will not relinquish control peacefully, is it justified to take up arms to overthrow that country's rule over your nation and regain independence?**

RV: I think sovereignty of the nation is a very important principle, and that it is a justification for uprising and resistance. I actually think it is interesting that by such criteria, resistance in Palestine against Israeli occupation would be justified.

**ED: What if another country with which you have treaty obligations is invaded?**

RV: If you have an agreement that an invasion of a particular country is a reason for war, and you've publicly stated that, then I think that that's an obligation.

**ED: That's how the United States got into Vietnam. At least, that's what was claimed, because we were part of SEATO (South East Asia Treaty Organization).**

RV: And that's a perfect example of why I think the theory is very different from the reality: because sometimes these treaties can be manipulated and used for reasons other than the ones for which they were intended. The United States got involved in Vietnam because of the Cold War with Russia, and Vietnam was essentially a client state of the U.S.S.R. The United States had an interest there and did more or less what it wanted and then found the legal justifications for doing so. Again, I think these questions are less interesting theoretically than they are when they're applied to actual circumstances.

**ED: What if another country in which you do not have any economic interests or treaty obligations is invaded by a third country that has threatened genocide? This would be, for example, Rwanda, Darfur ...**

RV: Kosovo.

**ED: Right. In other words, under those circumstances, if genocide is actually being committed or being threatened, is that a reason for a third country to go to war, in order to stop the genocide?**

RV: You know, this is a question that I'm very ambivalent about. I think, generally, the answer is yes. I think that, as a community of nations, we have an obligation to protect people, and that if genocide is genuinely threatened or is actually happening, there is an obligation to protect people across borders. I would be most comfortable seeing that happen through a body like the United Nations rather than through the actions of an individual country.

Again, because of the power issues that are at play, the United States, as a superpower, often undertakes actions selectively. It's never actually done anything militarily in terms of what's happened in Darfur, although it did intervene in the former Yugoslavia, for example. So I think that there are economic and political interests that often dictate whether a country takes action or not. Thus, I think it's very important to have an international consensus about what action to take in such circumstances and that such action be undertaken jointly rather than unilaterally. In the end, I would say it's justified and important to protect people from genocide.

**ED: What about a country in which the internal policies of the government lead it to commit genocide? So, for example, in Sudan, in which you have the Darfur situation, that's internal to the borders of Sudan.**

**RV:** Again, my answer to this is very similar to my answer to the previous question. I think the principle of protecting innocent civilians, whether they're in another country or in your own, is paramount. I would want proof both that genocide is happening and that other options for intervention have been tried and failed because, again, I think the principle of sovereignty—of one country respecting another—is important. Nevertheless, ultimately, if the situation met those levels of proof, then it's a necessary action to stop genocide anywhere it's happening.

**ED: Did you want to add anything more on the question of justifications for war?**

**RV:** Well, I think I just want to re-emphasize a couple of my primary points. One is that I think justification for war is very different from the conduct of war, and that both of those should be looked at. But they can't be looked at in isolation. Theoretically, you could start a war whose original reason is just, but then in its conduct it could become something that is really unjust. That being said, I think that, generally speaking, any time that a country enters into a war it needs to meet very, very high criteria in its reasons for waging that war, and it should always exhaust all other means before it turns to war as an option.

I'm somewhat uncomfortable, actually, with framing the discussion of war as a legal issue, as a decision that is not related to historic, economic, and political context. I want to say one thing on that point about the case of Israel specifically. I think that, when talking about war, it's extremely important to also take into consideration other factors.

Israel does not exist in a vacuum. It came into existence in a land that was already occupied and took it over, so all the things that led up to its wars, not just the immediate threats to which Israel was responding, do make a difference in determining the justness of those wars. Yes, you could say, for instance, that the Arab states "started" the war in 1948. However, the United Nations' partition plan was actually inherently unfair, given the imbalance in the number of Jews and Palestinians on the land and the fact that land was essentially being taken from the local population through the establishment of the State of Israel.

Moreover, the way the war was conducted, which resulted in the *nakhba* (the flight of Palestinian refugees during the War of Independence), which has shaped the conflict between Israel and Palestine until today, was in fact aggressive on Israel's part. And you could also say that Israel gained the territory additional to that which was set out in the partition plan by conquering land and essentially chasing out the local population.

So separating out justification for war from the conduct of war is problematic, as is looking at any war divorced from its larger political and historical circumstances.

# Case 3

# The Conduct of War

# Case Study

## A. Individual Conduct

Jason is a Jewish American soldier in his second year of army service. He is stationed in a foreign country in which the U.S. is engaged in military operations. He is 20 years old.

When Jason enlisted, he took an oath to obey the orders of his superiors, whom he respects for their experience in the battlefield. However, Jason is fearful—for his life and for his future career, even though he thinks that, by and large, his superiors know best how to preserve them both.

At the same time, Jason knows that the United States is a signatory to the Geneva Conventions, which establish internationally-recognized rules of war, but he is not very clear as to what they entail. He also has a sense that there are moral duties in all aspects of life, including war, that transcend international and military law. These include showing as much respect as possible for the value of life, even when facing an enemy on the battlefield, in accordance with the Jewish doctrine that each person is created in the image of God and deserves to be treated with dignity.

In light of international law, Jewish values, and the ethics that apply to military service, what would you advise Jason to do if the sergeant of his squad instructs him to do any of the following?

- break into a home in search of militants
- shoot anyone who comes out of a particular home
- throw a hand grenade at a school because militants are reported to be inside
- rape women in order to intimidate the enemy
- kill family members of militants to force them to come forward
- kill family members of militants, even if those being sought are dead
- torture suspects in order to get information from them
- torture suspects in order to humiliate and/or intimidate them

Jewish Choices, Jewish Voices: WAR AND NATIONAL SECURITY

## B. Military Conduct
If your country is engaged in war, should your military have the right to:
- engage in torture in order to elicit potentially life-saving information about an enemy's activities or plans?
- engage in targeted killings of leaders or members of enemy nations or organizations?
- take hostages with the intent of exchanging them for prisoners?
- engage in targeted bombing of military sites, even if it involves "collateral damage"?

Would your response to any of the situations mentioned above change if your country was responding to terrorist attacks instead of fighting in a declared war? What if war has not been explicitly declared against a country, but there are military operations taking place there, as in the Korean conflict in the 1950s or in Iraq in the 2000s?

## C. Non-Battlefield Conduct
In early 1948, prior to the formal establishment of the State of Israel, but during the time that the British were withdrawing, 35 Hebrew University students were sent to try to hold on to the Jewish settlement of Gush Etzion, southeast of Jerusalem. On their way, they met an old Arab shepherd. Because of his age and their need to move swiftly, they could not take him hostage; but they feared that if they did not kill him, he would alert the Arabs in the region that they were coming. Ultimately, they did not kill him, and he did alert the Arabs about them. As a result, all 35 were killed. Should they have killed the shepherd?

## D. Nuclear/Chemical Weapons
Was it right for President Truman to order that atomic bombs be dropped on Hiroshima and Nagasaki in 1945 in order to end the war with Japan, saving the lives of possibly hundreds of thousands of American troops, but at the expense of Japanese civilians? Would it be any different if World War II happened today and our President ordered chemical weapons to be used against the Japanese? What is the difference, if any, between using chemical or nuclear weapons and using conventional bombs or missiles?

# Traditional Sources

*Compiled by Uzi Weingarten and the Editors*

## The Conduct of War

### 1. Deuteronomy 20:10–14, 19–20

When you approach a town to attack it, you shall offer it terms of peace. If it responds peaceably and lets you in, all the people present there shall serve you at forced labor. If it does not surrender to you, but would join battle with you, you shall lay siege to it; and when the LORD your God delivers it into your hand, you shall put all its males to the sword. You may, however, take as your booty the women, the children, the livestock, and everything in the town—all its spoil—and enjoy the use of the spoil of your enemy, which the LORD your God gives you …

When in your war against a city you have to besiege it a long time in order to capture it, you must not destroy its trees, wielding the ax against them. You may eat of them, but you must not cut them down. Are trees of the field human to withdraw before you into the besieged city? Only trees that you know do not yield food may be destroyed; you may cut them down for constructing siegeworks against the city that is waging war on you, until it has been reduced.

### 2. Mishnah, *Sotah* 8:1

"Go out against your enemy" (Deuteronomy 20:1), and not against your brothers, not [the tribe of] Judah against [the tribe of] Shimon, nor [the tribe of] Shimon against [the tribe of] Judah, for [in the case of internal wars] if you fall into their hands, they will have mercy on you … [but rather] go out against your enemies, for if you fall into their hands, they will not have mercy on you.

### 3. Maimonides (Rambam), *Mishneh Torah*, Laws of Wars and Kings, 6:1, 7, 8

1. One does not wage war with anybody in the world before calling for peace, both wars of mitzvah and permitted wars, as it is written: "When you come near a city to wage war against it, call to it for peace" (Deuteronomy 20:1). If they surrendered and accepted the Seven Noahide Commandments, none of them is killed, and they become tributaries …

7. When laying siege to a city, one does not surround it on all four sides, but only on three sides, and one leaves a place for those who escape and those who run for their lives.

8. One does not chop down fruit-bearing trees outside the city, and one does not deny them water so that they wither, as it is written (Deuteronomy 20:19): "Do not destroy its trees."

## 4. *Sifra* on Deuteronomy 20:10, Parashat Shoftim 199

"[When you approach a town] to attack it"—and not to make it suffer starvation or thirst and not to make it die the death of sicknesses.

## 5. Deuteronomy 21:10–14

When you take the field against your enemies, and the LORD your God delivers them into your power and you take some of them captive, and you see among the captives a beautiful woman and you desire her and would take her to wife, you shall bring her into your house, and she shall trim her hair, pare her nails, and discard her captive's garb. She shall spend a month's time in your house lamenting her father and mother; after that you may come to [bed with] her and take her sexually, and she shall be your wife. Then, should you no longer want her, you must release her outright. You must not sell her for money: since you had your will of her, you must not enslave her.

## 6. Maimonides, *Mishneh Torah*, Laws of Wars and Kings, 8:1–2

1. Soldiers who enter foreign territory and capture it and take spoils may eat meat [that is not ritually slaughtered] and pork if they are hungry and do not find anything to eat other than these forbidden foods, and they may drink [non-kosher] wine. From the Oral Tradition we learn: "And houses filled with all good things" (Deuteronomy 8:1), pork and the like.

2. Similarly, a soldier [may] sexually take a gentile woman (ordinarily forbidden to a Jewish man) if his lust overcomes him. However, he may not sexually take her and leave, but rather he must bring her to his home, as it is written: "And you see among the captives a beautiful woman." And he may not sexually take her again until he marries her.

## 7. Babylonian Talmud, *Shabbat* 151b

Rabban Gamliel son of Rebbi says: Whoever shows mercy to people, Heaven has mercy on him. And whoever does not show mercy to people, Heaven does not have mercy on him.

## 8. Rabbi Yonah Gerondi (Spain, 13th century), *Sha'arei Teshuvah* 3:37, quoting *Yalkut Shimoni* 1 Samuel 121, *Midrash Shoher Tov* on Psalms 7

Whoever becomes merciful on the cruel ends up becoming cruel to the merciful.

# Contemporary Sources

*Compiled by Steven Edelman-Blank*

## The Conduct of War

### 1. Army Field Manual 1, Department of the Army, United States of America. Available at http://www.army.mil/fm1/index.html

1–58. The Army's culture promotes certain norms of conduct. For example, discipline is central to its professional identity. Soldiers, who manage violence under the stress and ambiguity of combat, require the highest level of individual and organizational discipline. Likewise, because Soldiers must face the violence of combat, they require the stiffening of discipline to help them do their duty …

1–59. Army norms of conduct also demand adherence to the laws, treaties, and conventions governing the conduct of war to which the United States is a party. The law of war seeks both to legitimatize and limit the use of military force and prevent employing violence unnecessarily or inhumanely. For Soldiers, this is more than a legal rule; it is an American value. For Americans, each individual has worth. Each is a person endowed with unalienable rights.

### 2. Ethics, Doctrine of the Israel Defense Forces. Available at http://dover.idf.il/IDF/English/about/doctrine/ethics.htm

Purity of Arms—The IDF servicemen and women will use their weapons and force only for the purpose of their mission, only to the necessary extent and will maintain their humanity even during combat. IDF soldiers will not use their weapons and force to harm human beings who are not combatants or prisoners of war, and will do all in their power to avoid causing harm to their lives, bodies, dignity and property.

3. **Reuven Kimelman, "The Ethics of National Power: Government and War from the Sources of Judaism,"** *Perspectives* **[February 1987], 15**

According to Israeli colonel Meir Pa'il, the "purity of arms" doctrine is able to maintain the moral stature of the soldier without seriously compromising his fighting capacity … There is a consistent thread weaving its way through Jewish ethical thought from biblical ordinance to modern practice as noted by ancient as well as medieval and modern observers. Just because an army is legitimately repelling an aggressor does not allow it recklessly to violate civilian life. A just war does not justify unjust acts.

4. *The Seventh Day: Soldiers Talk about the Six-Day War*, **Avraham Shapira and Henry Near, eds. (New York: Charles Scribner's Sons, 1970) [an English translation of** *Si'ah Lohamim, A Discussion of the Fighters,* **published in Hebrew in 1967], 67–68**

As we grew angrier, we stopped being human beings. You start out shouting, but by this time, we were all just machines for killing. Everyone's face is set in a snarl, and there's a deep growl coming from your belly. You want to kill and kill. You grow like an animal, you know—no, worse than an animal. Things were happening … I can't tell you about them. Once, one of our NCO's gave a drink of water to a prisoner. The Jordanian drank and then pulled a knife and slit the NCO's throat, like a chicken. Things like that. We killed the prisoner; you can't blame us. But you've got to understand what things like that did to us. We hated and hated. And all the time we were thinking what they would do to us and our families if they got us, and we were going along thinking, you're out for loot, are you? You'd rape my wife, my sister …

We didn't touch the civilians, though. You just don't think of civilians in the same way as soldiers. The soldiers, though, that's different. They don't seem like men to you. You don't think that they are people with families. You think all of the time of your own family, but *they* are just insects to be killed. Until afterwards, when you realize that they had families too …

5. **Michael J. Broyde, "Just Wars, Just Battles and Just Conduct in Jewish Law Is Not a Suicide Pact!" in *War and Peace in the Jewish Tradition*, Lawrence Schiffman and Joel B. Wolowelsky, eds. (New York: Yeshiva University Press, 2007). The Orthodox Forum Series, Series Editor, Robert S. Hirt, 7, 21–22**

Jewish law has no "real" restrictions on the conduct of the Jewish army during wartime, so long as the actions being performed are all authorized by the command structure of the military in order to fulfill a valid and authorized goal and do not violate international treaties. Sadly enough, it might turn out that most of these unpleasant activities we have considered might have to become tools in this quite gruesome *danse macabre* to which the long term consequences of defeat are too great to ponder. This is true both in the Jewish homeland and our beloved America …

Essentially Jewish law completely rejects the notion of a "siege" as that term is understood by military tacticians and contemporary articulators of international law. Modern international law generally assumes that in a situation where "the commander of a besieged place expel[s] the non-combatants, in order to lessen the number of those who consume his stock of provisions, it is lawful, though an extreme measure to drive them back as to hasten the surrender." Secular law and morals allow the use of the civilians as pawns in the siege. *The Jewish tradition prohibited that and mandated that non-combatants who wished to flee must be allowed to flee the scene of the battle* …

This approach solves another difficult problem according to Jewish law: the role of the "innocent" civilian in combat. Since the Jewish tradition accepts that civilians (and soldiers who are surrendering) are always entitled to flee from the scene of the battle, it would logically follow that all who remain voluntarily are classified as combatants, since the opportunity to leave is continuously present.

## 6. Abraham Joshua Heschel, "Required: A Moral Ombudsman" in *Moral Grandeur and Spiritual Audacity: Essays*, Susannah Heschel, ed. (New York: Farrar, Straus and Giroux, 1996), 219

To whitewash our deeds simply by maintaining our innocence is to defy God, who hears the cry of the guiltless killed in Vietnam. Jeremiah expressed it (2:14–15): "On your shirt is found the life-blood of guiltless poor. Yet in spite of all these things, you say: 'I am honest.' Behold I will bring you to judgment for saying: 'I have not sinned.'"

To offer easy forgiveness would be not only self-complacence but self-abasement. Easy forgiveness implies that an individual who has shot and killed men, women, and children is devoid of responsibility. Yet the individual's moral responsibility is the heart of the dignity of man. At a time of increasing dehumanization and mechanization of human existence, such an attitude would be a mortal blow to the humanity of man.

**Note:** Heschel wrote this essay in response to the conviction of Captain William Calley for his involvement in the My Lai Massacre.

## 7. Stanley Milgram, *Obedience to Authority: An Experimental View* (New York: HarperPerennial, 1974), 188–189

Each individual possesses a conscience which to a greater or lesser degree serves to restrain the unimpeded flow of impulses destructive to others. But when he merges his person into an organizational structure, a new creature replaces autonomous man, unhindered by the limitations of individual morality, freed of humane inhibition, mindful only of the sanctions of authority.

What is the limit of such obedience? At many points we attempted to establish a boundary. Cries from the victim were inserted; they were not good enough. The victim claimed heart trouble; subjects still shocked him on command. The victim pleaded to be let free, and his answers no longer registered on the signal box; subjects continued to shock him. At the outset we had not conceived that such drastic procedures would be needed to generate disobedience, and each step was added only as the ineffectiveness of the earlier techniques became clear …

The results, as seen and felt in the laboratory, are to this author disturbing. They raise the possibility that human nature or—more specifically—the kind of character produced in American democratic society, cannot be counted on to insulate its citizens from brutality and inhumane treatment at the direction of malevolent authority. A substantial proportion of people do what they are told to do, irrespective of the content of the act and without limitations of conscience, so long as they perceive that the command comes from a legitimate authority.

**Note:** This is the result of a famous experiment at Harvard University in which Milgram used students to demonstrate how people succumb to the pressures of authority.

## Non-Battlefield Conduct
### 8. Michael Gross, "Just and Jewish Warfare" in *Best Jewish Writing 2002*, Michael Lerner, ed. (San Francisco, CA: Jossey-Bass, 2002), 257

It cannot be denied that assassination has a great deal of intuitive appeal. It satisfies the need to strike back and to exact just punishment, long overdue and unattainable in any other way. Assassination is a source of pride, demonstrating Jewish military prowess as targets are picked off by the most imaginative means possible: booby-trapped cell phones, rigged automobiles, and rocket and tank attacks executed with almost pinpoint accuracy. Many claim that assassination prevents imminent terror attacks and serves as a powerful deterrent, giving potential terrorists pause while convincing Palestinian locals to distance themselves from terrorists. Finally, it is said, assassination accomplishes all this with minimal civilian casualties.

Assassination sounds like the perfect military tactic—and it would be, but for the fact that all these assumptions are naive, wrong, and entirely misguided. Assassination instead erodes the basis for any future peace negotiations, deters no one, and precipitates a violent, vicious, and almost insane desire for revenge.

## Nuclear/Chemical Weapons
### 9. Bradley Shavit Artson, *Love Peace and Pursue Peace: A Jewish Response to War and Nuclear Annihilation* (New York: United Synagogue of America, 1988), 220–221

The parallels between conventional warfare and nuclear combat are relatively straightforward. In both cases, national differences spill over [into] the realm of diplomacy and politics. Both involve killing members of the other society and, to some extent, attempting to minimize the damage suffered by enemy attacks. That is where the parallel ends. Beyond that, warfare serves a radically different purpose than does a nuclear exchange, and the kind of thinking involved in conventional warfare is very different from the type of planning necessary, and from the goals attainable through a nuclear conflict.

Albert Einstein once said that "I do not know what weapons will be used in the next war, but the one after that will be fought with bows and arrows." Even though his statement grossly underestimates the effect of an all-out nuclear war, it points to an important direction—toward the recognition that any proportionality of response is completely lost in a nuclear conflict. This is destruction without meaningful limits. That unlimited quality of warfare itself poses severe violations of the *halakhot* of warfare …

# Responses

## To Keep Our Honor Clean

Seth M. Milstein

JUSTIFICATIONS FOR war may be supported or undermined by the behavior of a nation's military (and other armed agents), which showcases the best or the worst of a nation's character on the harshest of stages. Soldiers are representatives of their nation and its foreign policy. In the realms of diplomacy, strategic communications, and public affairs, nothing speaks louder and more eloquently for a country than the actions of its armed services. How a nation wages war and how its soldiers conduct themselves, both in and out of combat, directly reflect both the ideals that nation stands for and the reasons why it opts to engage in war.

### War: What Is It Good For?

*It was around seven in the morning on March 20, 2003, when I was awakened by a jet engine roaring from north to south over my tent in Kuwait, just south of the Iraqi border. I had gotten to sleep a little after 4 a.m., following another long and painstaking night of planning for the invasion of Iraq that we all knew was imminent. The roar of the jet sounded awfully low, not at all like the sound of American airplanes, which occasionally flew overhead at very high altitudes. A thought crossed my still-fuzzy mind: "Either that's a Coalition airplane in big trouble, or ..." I got fully dressed, faster than I had ever done since Officer Candidate School many years previously, and I ran out of my small tent with my gas mask in one hand and my M-16 in the other.*

*I faced a group of young Marines pointing at the sky. A staff sergeant in the group was smiling as he said, "There go our tomahawks (missiles) on their way to Al-Faw (Peninsula, in southeast Iraq)."*

*I speared him with a look. I am not a morning person under the best of circumstances, and having my sleep cut short by an Iraqi missile, to start what promised to be the first of many very long days, did not help matters at all. I said, "Explain to me why missiles launched off ships would do a guided tour of the Kuwaiti desert on their way to coastal targets."*

*He paled as he blurted, "Sir, you mean we were just …"*

*I cut him off, "Yes, we've been fired on. Gents, we're officially at war with Iraq."*

War is an act of statecraft, where controlled violence is used to achieve national objectives. When statesmen and diplomats say, "Do (or don't do) this … or else," war is the most extreme "or else" available. As it is inherently wasteful, war is not an option to be considered lightly. War implies a degree of due process and reflects the character and spirit of the nation waging it. Democracies tend to be slow to go to war, except in times of crisis or when facing an imminent existential threat, but they tend to fight aggressively once public will is mobilized.

Nations need disciplined soldiers who apply no more and no less violence than necessary to meet strategic objectives. With effective discipline, soldiers learn to fight and to stop fighting as ordered, while using means that are consonant with the national character and support a military operation's overarching objectives. If the military uses means that are not congruent with national character, this undermines the legitimacy of an otherwise justifiable war. For example, while the first essential task in the United States National Security Strategy is to "champion aspirations for human dignity,"[1] nothing could be more incompatible with that strategy than the horrible, repugnant, and atypical conduct of a handful of U.S. soldiers at Abu Ghraib prison in 2004.

A common misconception is that the sixth of the Ten Commandments states, "You shall not kill." The Hebrew Scripture more correctly translates the commandment as, "You shall not murder." Thus, killing, while not a trivial matter, is justifiable as an act of statecraft, subject to due process and born of necessity. Due process is subject to a nation's governance, while necessity is framed by national and international politics. On an individual or a national level, self-defense can create the necessity for a violent, potentially deadly response. The absence of due process and necessity delegitimizes acts of violence, making killing, even by governments, murder.

---

1. From *The National Security Strategy of the United States of America* (Washington, DC: The White House, March 2006).

Case 3: Responses

## "Purity of Arms"

*The infantry fighting vehicle (IFV) crashed through the living room wall. About a dozen like it were deployed in a perimeter around the house. To most untrained observers, an IFV is frequently mistaken for a tank, but it differs from a tank in that instead of carrying vast numbers of shells for a large main gun, the hull has space for a squad of infantrymen. This IFV carried eight commandoes, who were already emerging from the rear hatch before pieces of the crashed wall had fallen off the vehicle's front slope armor. It took only seconds to find the master bedroom, confirm the identity of the surviving head of the Ba'ath party in Az Zubayr, Iraq from a photo, and drag him out of his bed, back to the IFV. The rear hatch had hardly closed when the IFV driver gunned the engine and drove through the wall on the other side of the house, back out onto the streets of Az Zubayr, which were otherwise quiet at three in the morning. The IFV turned sharply and joined the rest of the company, whose vehicles had collapsed the perimeter and formed into a single column lining the street. The vehicles roared away in a neat line, leaving the stunned townspeople to wonder who had hit with a combination of force and precision that Saddam Hussein's minions had never shown.*

A key concept in the thinking of the Israel Defense Forces (IDF), reflecting the character of the State of Israel, is Prime Minister David Ben-Gurion's doctrine of *tohar ha-neshek*, literally "purity of arms." Not surprisingly, and very similarly, American troops have two overarching guidelines for use of force: discrimination and proportionality.[2] To wit, efforts must be made to engage only appropriate targets, and to do so with a reasonable level of force. These subjective criteria are further defined by rules of engagement, intended to spell out those circumstances meriting the use of force, as well as appropriate levels of force. Discipline and leadership ensure that these moral and legal rules are respected and that suitable tactics are employed within the designated framework. For instance, deliberately targeting non-combatants and using excessive force are not acceptable.

Yet, the "purity of arms" doctrine does not rule out offensive action, as offense and defense are complementary and cannot be separated: imposing one's will upon the enemy is offensive, while resisting the

---

2. The discussion of discrimination and proportionality comes from *U.S. Army War College Guide to National Security Policy and Strategy*, J. Boone Bartholomees, Jr., ed., June 2006.

enemy's imposition of its own will is defensive. Being attacked first is not a necessary justification for defensive action. Preemptive action can be justified as self-defense if it is a response to a reasonable apprehension of imminent danger from a credible threat. Warfare varies with scale; an offensive action taken by a state is rather different from an offensive act committed by an individual soldier. Yet, there is no inherent contradiction in a national defense strategy that involves offensive military action. This is certainly the case for the United States, and also for Israel, where historically the blessings and curses of geography have repeatedly resulted in the need for preemptive action.

"Purity of arms" has become a more relevant principle as military technology has developed. As technology has increased the lethality and reach of weaponry, the "precision revolution" has given militaries a greater ability to attack legitimate targets while isolating surrounding populations from the destructive effects of such attacks more than ever before. Therefore, technological developments oftentimes allow military commanders to employ tactics that, while effective, are not deadly. This offers nations and their armed forces more options than just killing or doing nothing.

Today's unprecedented media coverage and its influence, post-engagement transparency about battlefield tactics, and use of propaganda by media-savvy enemies make it vitally important that countries are clear about their military intentions and policy, and ensure that their soldiers are acting in accordance with that policy. A guiding doctrine such as "purity of arms" provides the essential framework. The intrinsically political and increasingly public nature of war and its effects require that nations act on principle when engaged in military campaigns.

Innocents are, regrettably, sometimes caught in the crossfire or harmed by unpredictable consequences of warfare. Some argue that it is acceptable to use overwhelming force with little regard for collateral damage either to demonstrate resolve or to communicate in terms the enemy will understand. Such arguments, while pleasing at a visceral level, ignore that the means a nation uses to achieve a military goal reflect its national character. For instance, when the State of Israel was established, Ben-Gurion's *tohar ha-neshek* doctrine reflected the hope that the new nation would eventually make peace with its Arab antagonists, but trading atrocities in the name of military expedience does not help to accomplish that strategic goal. Similarly, America's Founding Fathers were not in favor of inflicting gratuitous suffering on the masses, and the spirit of the United States Constitution does not condone genocide or wanton killing. Resorting to heavy-handed and thuggish tactics flies in the face of the values that characterized the founding of the United States, such as freedom from oppression and tyranny.

**Ethics and the Individual Soldier**
*Three sergeants, each leading a reconnaissance team of four to six men, detailed their plans to observe a site believed to be the meeting place for four known terrorist cell leaders. Each man on this mission was to carry upward of 120 pounds of equipment and stealthily walk at least six kilometers from where a helicopter would drop him off, making speed and extraneous movement problematic.*

*"What if you are compromised while infiltrating your observation sites?" someone asked.*

*"We will silently kill individual terrorists and continue the mission, so long as they have been unable to report our presence," replied one sergeant.*

*"What if you are compromised by an elderly shepherd? He's not a terrorist."*

*"We'll tie him up, leave him in a shaded spot, and continue the mission," answered another sergeant.*

*"What if it's a little girl out picking mushrooms? Won't her family be concerned if she's gone for too long and come looking for her?"*

*"We'll hold her quietly to buy a few hours, to either exfiltrate or complete the mission, then let her go," was the answer.*

What does this incident reveal about the young and impressionable infantryman? He is taught to engage targets with as much discrimination as possible while judging what constitutes reasonable force. He has rules of engagement for each conflict (often written by lawyers for lawyers and frequently unclear to others) that provide further guidance on discerning acceptable targets and on related considerations, such as criteria for escalation of force. Discipline is a constant, whether it is imposed by his superiors or from within. The soldier is always accountable for himself and for the equipment and personnel in his charge. Regardless of the reasons leading to the war in which he is engaged or the nature of that war, his work environment is stressful, chaotic, and uncertain. He may be killed or injured by explosions or by being showered with fast-moving objects at any time, and he experiences the full gamut of human interactions with people whose language, culture, and circumstances are most likely unfamiliar to him. He spends much of his time dirty, sleep-deprived, hungry, in unpleasant climates, and under the constant physical strain of carrying and running with heavy equipment.

American military tradition imposes yet another burden on those in service: the obligation to disobey morally reprehensible or downright illegal orders. Although commanders may order their subordinates into potentially deadly situations, they may not order them to murder or rape noncombatants, to torture or kill prisoners, or to commit other atrocities. Commanders issuing such orders can expect refusal. Upholding the character of the United States, American military personnel swear first and foremost to "support and defend the Constitution," rather than to obey any political party, or even the armed forces itself.[3] This differentiates America's troops from those of most other nations, and it demands a high standard of ethics and judgment from the individual soldier. Although a soldier may not be an expert on international law and the conventions to which the United States is a party, if one's moral compass and common sense lead to the conclusion that he or she is being ordered to commit an atrocity, the soldier has a duty not to comply.

Given these underlying principles, the United States Armed Services have a tremendous responsibility for recruiting, training, and leading a certain caliber of soldier: recruits need to start with a strong moral compass, the wherewithal to assimilate what constitutes lawful and ethical practices, and the initiative to seek greater knowledge of those practices as they move into higher ranks and positions of greater responsibility. Commanders have an obligation to provide rules of engagement that are as clear-cut as possible and to conduct rigorous training that

---

[3]. The full oath for commissioned officers is: "I, (name), do solemnly swear (or affirm) that I will support and defend the Constitution of the United States against all enemies, foreign or domestic, that I will bear true faith and allegiance to the same; that I take this obligation freely, without any mental reservations or purpose of evasion; and that I will well and faithfully discharge the duties of the office upon which I am about to enter. So help me God." The full oath for enlisted men is: "I, (name), do solemnly swear (or affirm) that I will support and defend the Constitution of the United States against all enemies, foreign and domestic; that I will bear true faith and allegiance to the same; and that I will obey the orders of the President of the United States and the orders of the officers appointed over me, according to regulations and the Uniform Code of Military Justice. So help me God."

prepares soldiers to make hard choices under the inevitably stressful conditions of combat. Whenever possible, explaining the commander's intent and the reasons behind the rules enables better decision-making by subordinates.

Providing education about what constitutes unlawful or unethical behavior by talking out difficult scenarios under noncombat conditions is no less important. The classic example of such an exercise is figuring out what to do in a situation where a clandestine patrol is compromised by a noncombatant. This presents a challenge with no good solutions, but wrong answers aplenty for soldiers to think through. Ideally, commanders should also employ tactics to minimize the occurrence of real-life situations that force subordinates into ethical dilemmas. While this might be extremely difficult to achieve, the alternative is demonstrated in numerous cases where, given a range of tactical options, commanders have chosen poorly and left subordinates in terrible situations, forced to choose between bad and worse options on their own.

Thus, fielding a fighting force that is both effective and ethical is a tall order. The expectations of American officers are high, and every officer's commission decrees that the nation is "reposing special trust and confidence" in them.[4] Perhaps the hardest responsibility for officers, aside from overseeing the moral readiness of their charges and giving lawful orders, is providing oversight and appropriate disciplinary action when mistakes inevitably occur. In combat situations, where information is never perfect, bad decisions can be made in the heat of battle with tragic results. The chain of command needs to investigate such cases

---

4. The full wording on an American officer's commission reads: "To all who shall see these presents, greetings: Know ye that, reposing special trust and confidence in the patriotism, valor, fidelity, and abilities of (name) I do appoint this officer a (rank) in the (component of armed services) to rank as such from (date). This officer will therefore carefully and diligently discharge the duties of the office to which appointed by doing and performing all manner of things thereunto belonging. And I do strictly charge and require those officers and other personnel of lesser rank to render such obedience as is due an officer of this grade and position. And this officer is to observe and follow orders and directions, from time to time, as may be given by the President of the United States of America, or other superior officers acting in accordance with the laws of the United States of America. This commission is to continue in force during the pleasure of the President of the United States of America under the provisions of those public laws relating to officers of the Armed Forces of the United States of America and the component thereof in which this appointment is made." *Department of Defense Form 1 (1426)* (Washington, DC: Department of Defense, September 1999).

and determine if the implicated personnel were properly considering the information that they knew at the time, incorporating it into their analysis of the mission, and acting according to their moral compass. Hindsight may not be perfect, but justice demands consideration both of what the decision maker knew when he or she made a particular choice and of his or her intentions.

If a misguided moral compass or a craving for momentary emotional satisfaction overcomes discipline in some individuals, then officials have a duty to their nation and their army to deal with the culprits. The military is no place for sadists or bigots to live out their perverse fantasies—certainly not under the auspices of a national flag. It is needless to stoop to moral bankruptcy to inspire fear in enemies when legal means are plentiful. Soldiers need to be moral, disciplined individuals who can subordinate their natural emotions, such as hatred, fear, and outrage, and their cravings for vengeance, so that they may carry out their assigned responsibilities. Only then are they fit to be the agents a nation counts on to apply measured violence in accordance with the principles for which their country stands.

**Ticking Bombs, Torture, Targeted Killing, and Other Ethical Failures**
*On August 7, 1998, members of the Egyptian Islamic Jihad, a terrorist group associated with al-Qaeda, detonated truck bombs at the American embassies in Kenya and Tanzania, killing hundreds of civilians. This was the first time that Osama bin Laden came to the attention of the American public. On August 20, the U.S. Navy's 5th Fleet fired Tomahawk cruise missiles at al-Qaeda training camps in Afghanistan in an attempt to kill bin Laden and several of his closest associates. This effort proved to be a double failure: aside from missing bin Laden completely, the attack gave him a whole new level of legitimacy with his followers and potential friends. Until then, costly Tomahawk missiles had only been fired at military targets belonging to nations at odds with the United States. In the eyes of his admirers, firing the cruise missiles at bin Laden gave the relatively unknown terrorist leader prestige equal to that of an enemy nation of the U.S.*

The infantryman at war lives under constant threat of violent death or dismemberment or of seeing these things happen to his buddies. For him, this is like constantly living in a "ticking bomb" scenario. According to such a scenario, a "ticking bomb" is hidden in a major metropolis and heroic action is needed to stop it. Similarly, there is always a threat of imminent lethal violence on the battlefield, and the infantryman must take decisive action to defend himself and his fellow soldiers. Yet, he is also morally bound not to torture or kill every single civilian he meets, any of whom might have knowledge of the next attack. Military ethics and discipline also forbid him from torturing prisoners in his charge or engaging in other atrocities. The possibility of death or injury is a daily personal drama for thousands in a war zone, yet the need to stay within the bounds of ethical soldiering keeps the infantryman from giving in to his worst instincts. Those values for which a nation stands must remain more important than short-term expedience. It is hypocritical not to apply the ideals that soldiers are obliged to honor to the U.S. itself, even under circumstances of less imminent threat. Not asking citizens and the government to uphold these same ideals of due process, discriminate and proportionate use of force, and an aversion to oppressive and tyrannical methods, makes a complete sham of national character.

Torture is a truly effective tool for a police state. All but those with the strongest resolve will confess to anything, sign any document, and implicate anybody if they think it will get their tormentors to stop. As a means of gathering intelligence, however, torture is suspect at best, because those being interrogated will tell their questioners whatever they think they want to hear, factual or otherwise, to stop their own suffering. As with so many moral shortcuts, torture is quick, easy, and ultimately does not garner the same results as the slower approach to interrogation, which uses clever and sophisticated, but non-violent techniques. A Nazi Luftwaffe interrogator, Hanns Joachim Scharff, often called the greatest interrogator on record, used a technique that involved speaking with captive Allied aviators and outwitting them to obtain information without even threatening violence.[5]

By contrast, targeted killing, the precise elimination of a known and legitimate target, is almost the epitome of following the self-defense concept of *tohar ha-neshek* or the American precepts of discrimination and proportionality. A targeted killing is nothing more than a specialized ambush. A famous example is the interception and shooting down of Admiral Isoroku Yamamoto's airplane on April 18, 1943. Killing a specific enemy by circumventing his or her defenses protects lives. In

---

5. From Raymond F. Toliver, *The Interrogator* (Atglen, PA: Schiffer Military History, 1997).

contrast, a comprehensive, protracted engagement that might (or might not) kill the enemy target risks the lives of participating soldiers, as well as those of civilians and other bystanders.

This raises the basic question of what constitutes justifiable killing and points to the need for due process before employing force as statecraft. A soldier must establish that his target is, in fact, the one intended for destruction by making reasonable efforts to verify the identity of the target before attacking. Sending a large force to saturate an area risks greater numbers of casualties and more collateral damage, making it harder to justify than engaging a legitimate target with precision and control. Unless there is a strategic imperative that favors a particular method (and there are often sound reasons to consider alternative means of engagement to precise firepower), targeted killing is the more ethical military option.

## Conclusion

The actions of a nation's armed forces illustrate that nation's values. An army's responsibilities include recruiting, training, disciplining, and employing troops who wage war in a manner that reflects favorably on its country's character. The nation as a whole owes it to such an army to honor and live up to those same values that it expects its soldiers to support and defend. When soldiers are not faithful to the ideals upon which their country was built, and make emotional or convenient, but unethical choices in war, their nation may win battles, but it may lose the war, or worse, its soul.

Case 3: Responses

## Fighting, with Fear and Trembling

Sharon Brous

WITH BATTLE cries of, "Mission accomplished!," "Bring 'em on!," and "Dead or alive!," the early years of the 21st century have been marked by an aggressive American military strategy, most notably in Iraq, that has raised critical questions not only about the permissibility of warfare, but about the way in which war must be conducted.

In the heat of the Iraq War in 2007, upwards of 77% of American Jews said that they felt the war was a mistake, compared with 52% of the general American public who felt the same.[1] In light of Jewish tradition, this statistic is not surprising. The Talmud declares that "the whole Torah is for the sake of peace,"[2] arguing that the pursuit of peace is considered to be both a fulfillment of the Jewish people's mission in the world, as well as a way to make God's presence in our midst manifest.

Notwithstanding a general Jewish aversion to war, Jewish law does permit some types of war and even mandates that war be fought under certain circumstances. We are taught that abdication of personal or communal responsibility in the face of threats is both reprehensible and punishable. In the Babylonian Talmud we learn:

> Anyone who has the ability to protest against [the offenses of] the people of his house, but does not protest, that person is held responsible for the actions of the people of his house.

> Anyone who has the ability to protest against [the offenses of] the people of his city, but does not protest, that person is held responsible for the actions of the people of his city.

> Anyone who has the ability to protest against [the offenses of] the entire world, but does not protest, that person is held responsible for the actions of the entire world.[3]

Abandoning one's responsibility to fight in self-defense or against injustice is considered a grave moral failure.

---

1. Gallup Poll, February 2007. Available at http://www.gallup.com/poll/26677/among-religious-groups-jewish-americans-most-strongly-oppose-war.aspx.
2. Babylonian Talmud, *Gittin* 59b.
3. Babylonian Talmud, *Shabbat* 54b.

How are the commitment to peace and the obligation to fight reconciled? The great achievement of the Rabbis is that they devised an approach to warfare that mitigates its power and minimizes its devastation. Most notably, human dignity must remain an essential operating principle, so laws guiding the practice of warfare are embedded in a broader context of Jewish ethics. When war is fought, it must be fought with the utmost concern for the sanctity of human life, with an underlying commitment to humility, compassion, and even love.

**Principles of Waging War**

Given the essential commitment both to self-defense and to the defense of what is just and right, let us consider three examples of how war is to be initiated and conducted according to Jewish law. The first principle of war established by the Torah and reinforced by the Rabbinic tradition is that it must truly be a last resort. We are enjoined to work to exhaust all diplomatic options in an attempt to avoid violent conflict.[4] In the Torah, emissaries of peace are sent to hostile cities to search for any alternative to war.[5] If diplomacy ultimately proves unsuccessful, however, one is not permitted to attack unless the enemy initiates hostilities. And even then, one is forbidden to commit any acts of unwarranted cruelty against the inhabitants of enemy territory. Jewish law even goes so far as to require that an escape route be provided for those who desire to leave a besieged city at any point.[6] Permitting war only as a last resort minimizes the likelihood of violent engagement and creates a cultural aversion to warfare. War may be a necessary evil; it is never something to relish.

The second principle of warfare laid out in Jewish tradition is that war must be conducted in a way that preserves the humanity of the soldiers and civilians on both sides. This requires great moral sensitivity and vigorous protection against the dehumanization that typically characterizes warfare. Nahmanides (Ramban) taught that even the "most refined of people become possessed with ferocity and cruelty when advancing upon the enemy ... [Torah wants the soldier] to learn to act compassionately with our enemies even during wartime."[7] Part of the Jewish resistance to fighting is rooted in the humble awareness that more than life is lost in

---

4. Eg., see *Deut. Rabbah* 5:13.
5. Deut. 20:10.
6. Maimonides (Rambam), *Mishneh Torah*, Hilkhot Melakhim 6.
7. Nahmanides (Ramban), *Commentary on the Torah (Bi'ur)*, Deut. 23:10.

warfare—that violent conflict often comes with devastating moral compromise. In response to this moral challenge, nations that go to war must do everything in their power to ensure that their soldiers are trained with sensitivity and compassion, and that they are reminded, even amidst violent conflict, of the humanity of their enemies. In fact, the Torah offers specific rules intended to prevent the degradation of the enemy, even in the midst of dangerous conflict.[8] The assumption is that this moral training will ultimately preserve a soldier's own humanity as well.

A third guiding principle of war is the obligation to protect against unnecessary destruction—of human life, of the enemy's property, of the environment—during violent struggle. The call for soldiers to cultivate sensitivity toward the enemy renders wanton destruction thoroughly indefensible. "When in your war against a city," the Torah teaches, "… you must not destroy its trees, wielding the ax against them. You may eat of them, but you must not cut them down. Are trees of the field human to withdraw before you into the besieged city?" (Deut. 20:19–20). Maimonides (Rambam) extends this prohibition: "Also, one who smashes household goods, tears clothes, demolishes a building, stops up a spring, or destroys articles of food with destructive intent transgresses the command, *You shall not destroy*."[9] As Reuven Kimelman writes in his extensive treatment of the parameters of war from a Jewish perspective, "If one can control destructive urges provoked by war against nonhuman objects, there is a chance of controlling destructive urges against humans."[10]

**Translating Theory into Reality**

The question is: are these moral guidelines mere pollyanish abstractions, irrelevant in the face of enemies who commit brazen acts of violence against civilian populations? Perhaps the guidelines were always intended to be only theoretical, considering that it is questionable whether the Rabbis who helped create them "*ever* had a sovereign construct in which their guidelines for war were operationalized."[11]

---

8. Eg., see Deut. 21:10.
9. Maimonides (Rambam), *Mishneh Torah*, Hilkhot Melakhim 6:10.
10. Reuven Kimelman, "War," *Frontiers of Jewish Thought*, Stephen Katz, ed. (Washington, DC: B'nai Brith Books, 1992), 315.
11. Marc Gopin, *Between Eden and Armageddon* (New York: Oxford University Press, 2000), 72.

If that is indeed the case, would application of these principles be dangerously naïve in circumstances where there are people calling for the destruction of the State of Israel or seeking to strike the United States with the intention of killing as many civilians as possible? Would an adherence to traditional Jewish principles on warfare ultimately render a nation incapable of defending its citizens and of ensuring its own continued existence?

A core commitment to the preservation of humanity—our own and that of our enemies—means that we do not shy away from protecting ourselves, our civilians, and our values, but that when we fight, we do so not with bombast and arrogance, but with fear and trembling. We never delight in the opportunity to fight, and we work to ensure that our soldiers' conduct in war lives up to the highest possible standards of moral decency. The fact that a nation may have a legitimate need to fight does not justify recklessness. In the words of Martin Buber:

> … what matters is that in every hour of decision we are aware of our responsibility and summon our conscience to weigh exactly how much is necessary to preserve the community, and accept just so much and no more … that we do not salve, or let others salve our conscience when we make decisions concerning public life.[12]

In the Book of Genesis, Abraham emerges victorious after fighting the invading armies of four mighty kings. In his first moment of rest after the battles, he is addressed by God: "*Al tirah Avram—Fear not, Abram*" (Gen. 15:1). But why would Abraham be afraid? He has just vanquished his enemies and is, for the first time in years, able to dwell in peace. The Rabbis teach that his fear derived from a persistent post-war apprehension, as he thought, "Perhaps there was *one* righteous or God-fearing person among the people I killed."[13]

What would that kind of moral sensitivity look like in our time? The hour calls for a heartfelt reaffirmation of our shared humanity—something that seems to have been lost in contemporary warfare. Perhaps that will help us step out of the morass of these violent times and begin to build pathways toward peace.

---

12. Martin Buber, *Israel and the World* (New York: Schocken Books, 1948), 246.
13. *Bereshit Rabbah* 15:1.

Case 3: Responses

# Ethics on the Battlefield

Joe Kashnow

MAINTAINING THE moral high-ground while using deadly force might seem impossible. Yet, American fighting men and women have proven that we can act with decency and morality in combat missions and, at the same time, maintain an effective fighting force that is able to accomplish its goals. This is not easy to do, however. As Americans have seen on a few occasions in recent history, some members of our military have fallen short of the goal to behave honorably. Even so, it is important to be clear that those moral lapses represent isolated incidents, and that the actions of a few individuals do not represent the behavior of the military at large.

## My Experience as a Soldier at War

I served in Iraq for six months, from April through September of 2003, where I witnessed soldiers act with a sense of honor that I found to be truly amazing. I served as a prison guard for a few men who were captured after a failed assault on one of my battalion's patrols. The sergeant in charge of giving my squad instructions was the vehicle commander during the assault, which had happened the night before. Both of his crew members, his driver, and his gunner were wounded and had to be flown out of the country for emergency medical treatment. The gunner was in particularly bad shape, and it was not clear if he would even live long enough to get back to the United States. Despite the attack, despite holding his driver's head together while the medic bandaged him, despite being wounded himself, that sergeant gave me and the other guards crystal clear orders that left no doubt as to the punishment that we would receive should those prisoners who perpetrated the assault be mistreated in any way.

I remember the medic who, while on patrol, was shot in the chest by a sniper. He was wearing his ballistic armor and survived the attack with no more than a bruise. When the ensuing firefight was over and the sniper was discovered not to have been killed but only to have been wounded, that same medic bandaged the sniper and called for a helicopter so that the patient could get the medical treatment he so desperately needed.

There are times, however, when the line of moral behavior gets extremely blurred. The overriding concept that most soldiers believe in is simply: "my life is more important than anyone else's because it is my own life." In regard to other people's private property, however, it is acceptable to enter someone's home and search for weapons, explosives, and any other contraband. Why? Only because we do it carefully, taking measures not to risk lives.

I have led squads of soldiers on home raids, with mixed results. All of my soldiers understood that they were not to simply trash a house when searching it. My soldiers in Iraq knew that every drawer of every cabinet in someone's home was to be opened, but then put back after the entire cabinet had been searched, without dumping the contents on the floor. They also knew how to search a closet without throwing everything around. Most often when we found nothing, the owners of the house thanked us as we were leaving.

On one occasion, however, I was accused of stealing jewelry from a home where we had found a supply of more than 100 car batteries on the porch. At that time, car batteries were used as a crude power supply for detonating roadside bombs. After asking the woman who lived there when her husband would be home, she accused me of stealing from her. Interestingly, I was also the translator during this conversation, and because of that, I had been standing next to our battalion commander the entire time we were there and had not stepped foot inside her house. That was one house where my battalion was not thanked as we left.

Sometimes, though, soldiers get bad intelligence; for example, we may be given a tip by someone who has a personal grudge against a family and wants to see them harmed or inconvenienced. Dealing with a populace that is not able to get along with one another is inherently dangerous. Remembering to be respectful of other people as well as cautious can mean the difference between life and death in a war zone. A family that is treated with care by a search team may be willing to provide crucial intelligence in the future. A family that was effectively terrorized or humiliated by a search team is likely to cheer when the next American convoy is ambushed.

## Unacceptable Wartime Conduct: Rape and Torture

There is a significant difference between invading someone's town or home and invading someone's body. Rape, when used as a tool to inspire fear or intimidation, is arguably effective. Of course, there is the counter-argument that it can anger an enemy, leading it to be more motivated than it was before; but when the goal is to cause fear, rape is usually a more effective tool than murder. Yet, this behavior is unconscionable and completely unacceptable. There are few actions that may never be used under any circumstances in war, and rape is one of them.

We all know that torture is wrong, and yet if my child were missing and I knew that using the cattle prod in an interrogation would elicit the information necessary to save his or her life, I would definitely use it. The question about torture is not whether it is a viable means of intelligence-gathering, but if it is acceptable to intentionally inflict pain on another human being to get that person to reveal information that he or she may be withholding. Even if that information would save a life, most people would still say that using torture to extract it is wrong.

But the line becomes blurred as weapons become more powerful. What if the subject knows the code to disarm a bomb that is located in an elementary school? What if that bomb is a nuclear weapon? What if it is a device designed to poison the water supply of an entire region? How many people could we watch die before we allowed ourselves to violate this one person?

Perhaps the most compelling reason not to use torture, though, is because it is unreliable. People will often say what they think someone wants to hear if it will make the pain stop. Thus, maybe just the threat of torture can be used effectively. However, if, for example, three people sit in a jail cell and then the first two are taken away, allowing the last person to get a good earful of the others' screams, that would be a very effective way to encourage him or her to talk. While that is not inflicting pain directly on the subject, that would likely cause his or her will to break. Any tactic that accomplished breaking someone so cruelly could be said to be torture. There is a difference, though, between hurting and humiliating people for entertainment and using effective measures to interrogate a subject with intelligence vital to a military mission.

While Iraq was under Saddam Hussein's control, for instance, there was cruel and unjustified torture in that country. Truly terrifying acts of barbarism would end only when a prisoner stopped holding on to the belief that at some point he or she might be freed or believed innocent, and ultimately died. I saw rooms that had evidence of that type of torture—

true torture. Often it had been performed only to entertain the guard and to terrorize other captives who were forced to watch just so they would be stripped of hope. There is no validity to the argument that "we must be right because 'they' were so much worse." We must ask: does inflicting pain on someone just to scare him or her or other prisoners count as torture? If it does, it should be banned.

During the wars in Korea and Vietnam, captured American service members were often tortured in ways that are indescribable. They would sometimes be put into tanks filled with water in an attempt to simulate drowning. Often this practice would go beyond simulation, and the prisoners would be killed. Scaring someone into talking is not torture, it is effective interrogation. Letting a prisoner die because he or she won't talk is murder, and when it is done in a painful manner, then it is torture.

**Ethical Conduct on the Battlefield**

Superior technology may help a military effort, but boots on the ground are the critical element of any military operation. When soldiers are deployed with weapons and ammunition, someone is going to get killed. However, American soldiers' permission to fire is so restricted that it almost renders our fighting force ineffective. I have heard other American soldiers complain too many times to count that we are fighting today's conflicts with our hands tied behind our backs.

There is a good reason for such restrictions, though. We restrict our forces' conduct to minimize the deaths of the innocent. When taking fire from a schoolhouse where there are children present, we do not return fire. When a terrorist uses a crowd of people as a shield to fire a rocket at an American vehicle, we do not shoot indiscriminately into the crowd. To prevent shooting people who appear to be charging an American convoy, we fire warning shots into the air before shooting at them, even though they or their vehicle may turn out to be wired with a bomb. We do not open fire on someone just because he or she walked through a door that leads to a known terrorist compound on the off chance that, this time, this individual is not armed. We do not capture the family members of a known terrorist and execute them one by one on television in order to get the terrorist to come out of hiding.

We do not do these things because there are certain standards of conduct that are required of the United States as the world's superpower. As

Americans, we must behave in a manner that is above reproach. We have been accused of being overly arrogant in our military operations, but there is little to support that claim. We went into Iraq to remove a dictator that tortured his own people. Saddam Hussein was more than willing to use weapons of mass destruction against Iraqis and was actively searching for ways to make those weapons. His government was also a state sponsor of terrorism. As the world's policeman, it has become the United States' responsibility to protect the rights of people everywhere, and thus, the U.S. military must intervene in places like Iraq if it is to keep the world safe.

# Rules for War
Ari Brochin

## Controversial Actions: Sharon and Kuntar

ON OCTOBER 15, 1953, Ariel Sharon led an Israel Defense Forces commando unit in an assault on the village of Kibya in what was then the Jordanian-occupied West Bank. Fed up with terrorist attacks on Israeli civilians, the Israeli government had turned to Sharon to ensure that the Palestinians, as a whole, "paid a heavy price."[1] Sharon and his unit fought their way into the village and proceeded to blow up 45 homes as well as a school and a mosque. At least 69 civilians were killed in these explosions, many of whom were hiding from the Israelis in their houses. Sharon later claimed that he had no idea there were people in those houses. The assault was condemned by the world community, and when Sharon became Israel's Prime Minister decades later, it was widely cited in newspaper articles as the reason for Sharon's reputation among Palestinians for extreme violence.

The return of Samir Kuntar to Lebanon got me thinking of Ariel Sharon. Kuntar is one of the most notorious killers in the name of the Palestinian cause. In 1979, at the age of 16, Kuntar was a member of the terrorist cell that murdered, among others, three members of the Haran family of Nahariya, Israel. Kuntar killed Danny Haran in front of his four-year-old daughter, then smashed the girl's skull with a rifle butt. The Haran's other child was accidentally smothered by her mother while hiding from the terrorists. Israel arrested, tried, and imprisoned Kuntar, a Lebanese citizen. In 2006, Hezbollah cited Kuntar's continued imprisonment as justification for the assault that provoked the Israel–Lebanon war.

In the summer of 2008, Kuntar was returned to Lebanon along with other prisoners, in exchange for the bodies of two Israeli soldiers. His return was celebrated as a national holiday there, and a hagiographic documentary on Kuntar aired on Al-Jazeera television. Like many observers, I was disgusted when I heard news reports of the celebrations held for Kuntar in Lebanon and throughout the Arab world. The emotions I saw being expressed were as foreign to me as anything I had ever witnessed. It seemed like the

---

1. Flore de Préneuf, "An Eye for an Eye," *Salon,* Feb. 6, 2001.

entire Lebanese nation believed that it was laudable to crush the skulls of toddlers, so long as those toddlers were from the appropriate country.

I grew up on the political Left, but in recent years, I have become disaffected with the refusal of a vocal core of progressives, in my social circle and in the media, to recognize that a proper moral calculus on the Middle Eastern conflict is not made simply by determining which side ought to be given credit for anti-colonialism. Nonetheless, I still identify with a central insight of American progressivism: that people, including Jews, Zionists, and Americans, are predisposed to drawing moral lines that condone the behavior of those like themselves and condemn that of those who are different. I tried to figure out if my moral judgment of Samir Kuntar, and those who celebrated his exploits, was based on my identification with his victims, or on a feeling that his actions were, even with my particular identification removed, absolutely wrong. I tried to think of a situation in which a Jewish killer of innocent Arabs was treated as a hero. I thought of Kibya and Ariel Sharon, and of the analysis of one of Israel's greatest thinkers, Yeshayahu Leibowitz.

### Leibowitz's Analysis

Shortly after the assault on Kibya, Professor Yeshayahu Leibowitz, Israel's preeminent public intellectual from the birth of the state until his death in 1994, wrote an article entitled "After Kibya."[2] In the article, he spoke of Kibya as a symbol of the responsibility that Jews had avoided in the Diaspora, but that they were given, or forced to assume, with the birth of the State of Israel. As long as Jews lived in the homelands of other peoples, they were oppressed and excluded, often as individuals but always as a community, from decision-making power. Jews were free to regard abhorrent actions by agents of the states in which they lived as the strange behavior of the gentile other.

To Leibowitz, Zionism meant that the ethical decisions that had been easy for Jews because they had so often been kept out of the decision-making process, were no longer easy. Because civilians were now being attacked in the name of the security of a *Jewish* state, Jews finally had to make ethical decisions in the context of their own military policy. Thus, Leibowitz did not frame the moral issue evoked by the Kibya attack as

---

2. Yeshayahu Liebowitz, "After Kibya," *Beterem*, Dec. 15, 1953.

a matter for the personal consciences of the individual participants, but rather as a challenge to his sense of national political morality.

I believe that there is a great deal of wisdom in Leibowitz's approach, but that it is incomplete. It is important to judge the political morality of Ariel Sharon and Samir Kuntar. It is also important to judge the morality of each action of individual soldiers who are insulated from the political decision-making process that brought them into battle. The actions of individuals who are charged with carrying out a collective political act for their state reflect the values that society teaches. Unless those individuals are clearly rejected by their fellow citizens, their actions ought to be judged primarily as a realization of the political will of their community. Therefore, the ethical decisions that are a necessary part of conflict are made on both an individual and a collective level, neither of which can be divorced from the other.

**Battlefield Ethics: The Citizen's Role**

On the level of personal morality, Sharon and Kuntar's choices lend themselves to a moral discourse that is reduced to banalities. It seems obvious that individuals should not blow up the houses of civilians, particularly when civilians are inside, and even more obvious that intentional and brutal infanticide is wrong. The fact remains, though, that both Sharon and Kuntar have their defenders. For the sake of soldiers like the one in the case study, Jason, and of the leaders and societies that send them off to battle, the banalities that constitute the basic ethics of the battlefield bear repeating.

However, a part of me hesitates to give advice to soldiers and military planners tasked with morally difficult work. Although I believe that it is important that citizens help to establish norms of battlefield ethics, we must do so with a sense of humility. I have never had a friend enlist in the American armed forces. This reflects a general abdication of the responsibility of military service among my cohort of educated, liberal Jews. This situation leaves only two morally viable options: support of absolute pacifism, or some degree of deference to and sympathy for those who have chosen to put their lives at risk in service of our country.

Yeshayahu Leibowitz would appreciate the irony of the tension that I feel. American Jews live in a country where there are no legal restrictions on their participation in any aspect of society, yet the Jews in my social circle have universally chosen not to enroll in the armed forces. They have thus chosen to leave some of the morally difficult work of self-governance disproportionately to non-Jews. I can think of no reason why liberal educated Jews have less of an obligation to serve in the military than do other citizens. When American Jews abdicate a responsibility of citizenship, we confirm Leibowitz's contention that the Jews of the Diaspora are not fully responsible political actors. It is impossible to square my belief that the burdens of democracy should be shared equally with the position that I and my community have taken. But even as I recognize that many in the Jewish community have abdicated the important responsibility of military service, I feel an obligation to participate in American, and Jewish American, conversations about battlefield morality.

## One Basic Principle of Battlefield Ethics
Leibowitz would also appreciate that the most immediate way for me to enter such conversations is through analyzing incidents in the history of the State of Israel—a place where Jews are more commonly the perpetrators and victims of violence. So, as an ambivalent American Jewish Zionist, here is what I think Jason can draw from the examples of Ariel Sharon and Samir Kuntar: Sharon's actions were not as morally reprehensible as those of Kuntar, but that does not excuse them.

Both Sharon and Kuntar claimed that they were not responsible for the acts attributed to them. Kuntar claimed not to have killed the Harans, but never offered an even superficially convincing alternative explanation for their deaths, while Sharon claimed that he had no idea that people were hiding in the houses he ordered blown up. In the world of civilian criminal law, Sharon's excuse would not count for much. Setting off 47 explosions with the intent to demolish buildings without first establishing that no one is inside, killing 69 people in the process, is close to a textbook definition of murder through recklessness and extreme indifference. Both Sharon and Kuntar intentionally targeted civilians and acted without regard for the goal of reducing the military capabilities of an enemy.

The actions of both were wrong, but Kuntar's actions were especially wrong because of the first banal but often ignored rule that should guide Jason's actions:

> **Do not intentionally kill civilians when doing so is not directly required to achieve a specific and vitally important goal.**

According to such a guideline, I cannot get away from my basic moral judgment that, while Sharon's conduct was wrong, Kuntar's actions were far worse. One major moral difference between the acts of Sharon and the acts of Kuntar was in their goals. Sharon's team was sent on its mission in the wake of terrorist attacks on Israeli civilians. His mission had two objectives. The first was to display a show of force by the Israeli army that would lead to a reduction in terrorist attacks against Israeli civilians. The second goal was to show that the spilling of Jewish blood would not go unavenged.

Samir Kuntar's attack was an act of political protest, specifically against the Camp David peace accords between Israel and Egypt, and more generally against the existence of the State of Israel. It was not calculated to bring about any specific or immediate political change. Therefore, unlike Sharon, Kuntar had no reasonable purpose or justification for what he was doing, rendering his entire mission immoral. Given the lack of any specific or important goal, his actions would have been immoral even if he had only engaged in acts that are often morally justifiable in war, like targeting soldiers, instead of citizens, with violence.

Sharon, in contrast, set out to achieve a legitimate goal. The problem was with the method he chose to pursue it. It was wrong for Sharon to destroy the houses in Kibya, and even more wrong for him not to make sure that no civilians were inside of them. Jason should not emulate his actions.

### A Second Basic Principle of Battlefield Ethics

It is worth noting, however, that soldiers like Jason often do not know why they have been given their orders. The orders Jason might receive—to shoot people coming out of a particular house, to break into a particular home, to assault a particular school—may or may not be moral, depending on whether military necessity outweighs the risk of harm to civilians. Even though Jason is the one acting, he is not the moral decision maker. Yet, it is appropriate for him to scrutinize the moral judgments of those determining battlefield tactics. Jason's moral role as a soldier is limited to those judgments that he is informed enough to make, but those who launch military strategies must have the knowledge to make moral decisions about what Jason and his fellow soldiers are ordered to do on the battlefield.

While Ariel Sharon and Samir Kuntar were the commanders of their operations, their actions as soldiers—making decisions in the moment of battle—are more relevant to Jason. The rule that Kuntar clearly violated, and that Sharon violated to a lesser extent, is one that Jason should obey in that moment:

**Do not do anything that is obviously unspeakably horrible.**

This rule is perhaps the most difficult to articulate, but the easiest to feel, and it highlights the ultimate moral difference between Sharon and Kuntar's actions. Kuntar killed a small child with his own hands, using particularly bloody means. Sharon killed children recklessly but indirectly. Both acts resulted in the deaths of children, and Sharon's killed more children. Nonetheless, Kuntar's acts *feel* far worse than Sharon's. There is just something about that image of a teenager smashing the skull of a toddler that speaks of evil in a way that the image of Sharon's calculated, goal-oriented destruction of civilian property and his reckless killing of scores of civilians does not.

Obviously, training soldiers means forcing them to put aside some of their moral compunctions, but there are some things that no cause can justify. Kuntar's act provides one vivid example. The message here for Jason is that he must refrain from killing the unarmed, and from the use of rape, sexual humiliation, or torture, which are all immoral acts that are obviously unspeakably horrible.

Ultimately, most moral decision making will be made above the level of the individual soldier. Jason and his colleagues will, hopefully, be trained and commanded by morally engaged superiors who give clear, specific instructions regarding what is morally and legally permissible. The possibility remains that Jason will encounter insufficient oversight, or morally deficient leadership. In this situation, the best advice I have to offer him is this: try not to be like Ariel Sharon, but never, ever be like Samir Kuntar.

## Does Torah Permit Torture? Defending Dignity, Life, and Sacred Personhood[1]

Melissa Weintraub

GUANTANAMO BAY detention camp, circa 2002: Men are in dog leashes, being forced to perform dog tricks and wear lacy lingerie on their heads. Female interrogators dressed in skimpy mini-skirts are straddling the laps of traditional Muslim men, rubbing their breasts against the men's backs, and wiping red dye they passed off as menstrual blood on the men's faces. Some detainees are being taunted with vicious dogs to scare them, others bombarded with painfully bright lights and loud violent music, left naked in isolation, hooded, spat on, urinated on, exposed to extreme cold to the point of induced hypothermia, and deprived of food and sleep.[2]

Torture joins slavery as one of the practices most unanimously condemned in international law, as well as in the domestic laws of most nations, including the United States. Nevertheless, from Hollywood to Capitol Hill, our post-9/11 nation has posited torture as a subject for moral equivocation. May torture—or milder related practices—ever be deemed permissible? Is the use of torture an unseemly but necessary outcome of the state's right and responsibility to protect its citizens from terror?

In this essay, I will interrogate rationales for torture from the perspective of Jewish ethics in order to argue for an absolute proscription against torture. My essay will pivot on two principles in Jewish law, twin commandments granted priority over many other religious obligations, namely: the imperative to honor the dignity of the human person, viewed as being created in God's image; and the kindred, but at times conflicting obligation to defend human life at great cost. The question of the permissibility of torture throws into relief both the tension between these two principles and their inextricability, for they mutually rest on a concept of human personhood as a sacred and inviolable trust from God.

---

1. A previous version of this article appeared in the Summer 2007 edition of the *Review of Faith & International Affairs* and in *Torture is a Moral Issue: Christians, Jews, Muslims, and People of Conscience Speak Out*, George Hunsinger, ed. (Grand Rapids, MI: Eerdmans, 2008).
2. See for example, "Detainees Accuse Female Interrogators: Pentagon Inquiry is Said to Confirm Muslims' Accounts of Sexual Tactics at Guantánamo," *Washington Post*, Feb. 10, 2005, A01. For additional references, see Melissa Weintraub, "Kvod Ha-Briot: Human Dignity in Jewish Sources, Human Degradation in U.S. Military Detention," 1–11. Available at http://rhr-na.org/torture/tortureresources.html.

Case 3: Responses

## *Kevod ha-Beriyot:* **Human Dignity in** *Halakhah*

*The most fundamental assumption of Jewish ethics is that there is something intrinsically and ineradicably sacred about the human person, the human body and spirit as such.*

The ontological fact of our collective creation in God's image enjoins us to moral behavior, commanding us to work actively to honor the lives and dignity of other human beings. This idea that the human being is created *b'tselem Elohim*, in the image of God originates in the first chapter of the book of Genesis.

On the basis of this assumption, Judaism formulates a prohibition against violations of human dignity. Classical Jewish literature refers to human dignity by the term *kevod ha-beriyot*—the dignity of "*created* beings" rather than the dignity of "*human* beings"—grounding the requirement to protect dignity in the divine origins of the human. On the basis of this concept, early Rabbinic commentary presents debasement of humans, even as a retaliatory act, as an outrage against God.

Human dignity is arguably the foundational and most aspirational ideal of Jewish law. The injunction to avoid humiliating or contemptuous behavior takes legal precedence over all other Rabbinic rulings.[3] The Rabbis thus designate human dignity as the litmus test for their sacred law, a seeming recognition that were the law to participate in dishonoring the human person, it would betray its own *raison d'etre*.

What are some of the practical implications of this lofty principle?

1. *We are not to debase the human body.* For many authorities, the idea that the human body is the corporeal representation of divinity gives rise to legal prohibitions against tattooing and multiple piercings,[4] not only outright abuse and degradation of the body.

---

3. See Babylonian Talmud, *Berakhot* 19b; *Shabbat* 81a-b, 94b; *Eruvin* 41b; *Megillah* 3b; *Bava Kamma* 79b; *Menahot* 37b, 38a. The parallel text in the Jerusalem Talmud (JT) presents the opinion of R. Zeira that even Torah commandments are temporarily overridden where they conflict with human dignity (JT Kil. 9:1). The JT seems to consent to R. Zeira's opinion, citing it in another context to demonstrate that a Torah obligation may indeed be set aside for the sake of human dignity (JT Nazir 7:1 [56a]; JT Ber. 3:1). For an overview of this concept in Jewish law, see Nahum Rakover, "The Protection of Human Dignity," *Jerusalem City of Law and Justice*, Ravoker, ed., Library of Jewish Law, 210–211.
4. See Alan Lucas, "Tattooing and Body Piercing," *Yoreh De'ah* 180 (1997), *Responsa of the CJLS 1991–2000*. Available at http://www.rabbinicalassembly.org/teshuvot/docs/19912000/lucas_tattooing.pdf.

The law prohibits dishonoring even the dead body of a criminal convicted of a capital crime.[5]

2. *We are not to shame others through demeaning speech, threats, or insults.* Doing so is conceived of as a form of violence akin to murder. The Talmud states that, "He who publicly shames his fellow is as though he shed blood," and describes the act of shaming as "whitening the face"—turning another into a living corpse. Shaming, teaches the Talmud, constitutes an *irreparable* wrong because it permanently injures another's personhood.[6]

Whose humanity is worthy of such honor? May one forfeit the right to dignified treatment? The sources teach us that the obligation to treat others with dignity and avoid shaming is not conditional on what sort of person someone is. For instance, the Talmud voices anxiety over the inevitable humiliation involved in arrest before a person, presumed innocent, has been convicted through due process of law.[7] The texts present the criminal offender's dignity, even post-conviction, as intrinsic to his humanity, independent of his personal attributes and actions.

The Israeli Supreme Court extends these *halakhic* (Jewish legal) concepts to contemporary, concrete cases involving the rights and dignity of prisoners. Citing the principle of *kevod ha-beriyot* (human dignity), the Israeli High Court has determined in several landmark decisions that prisoners must be provided with all of their basic human needs and treated as civilized people:[8]

> A free and civilized society is distinguished from a barbaric and oppressive society by the degree to which it treats a human being as

---

5. Deut. 21:23, Rashi ad. loc.
6. Babylonian Talmud, *Bava Metzi'a* 58b–59a.
7. Jerusalem Talmud, *Sanhedrin* 7:10. Cf. Maimonides, *Mishneh Torah, Hilkhot Sanhedrin* 24:10.
8. "It is firmly entrenched in our law that the fundamental rights of man 'survive' also behind prison walls, and are granted to the prisoner (and the detainee) also in his prison cell." See Prisoner's Petition Appeal 4463/94, *Golan v. Prison Service, Piskei Din (Israeli Case Report)* 50(4) 136, at 152–153. Cf. the comments of the Vice-President of the Supreme Court, Haim Cohen: "It is the right of a person in Israel who is sentenced to imprisonment (or who is lawfully detained) to be incarcerated in conditions that allow him to live a cultured life," High Court of Justice 221/80, *Darwish v. Prisons Service*, ibid., 538.

a human being ... Just as the [talmudic] rabbis were bold enough to waive all prohibitions instituted by them where necessary to preserve human dignity, [our law] should be cautious in sacrificing human dignity on the altar of any other requirement whatsoever.[9]

Citing the overriding importance of human dignity, the Israeli Supreme Court categorically outlawed torture and cruel, inhuman, and degrading treatment in 1999—including specific methods that became prevalent in U.S. military detention after 2001. The court rejected the logic implicit in the Bush administration's invented category of the "enemy combatant," that the "terrorist" forfeits the protections inherently granted to all other human beings. It determined, rather, that Israel's agents must "preserve the human image" and dignity of even those detainees known to be directly involved in terror activities, including suicide bombings.[10]

## But Does Torture Save Lives? The Jewish Counter-Argument

Torture cannot be repudiated on grounds of human dignity without reckoning with the other and still weightier moral and legal obligation of Jewish tradition. For alongside the injunction to safeguard human dignity on the basis of sacred human personhood, we are enjoined by a sometimes competing positive obligation to defend human life at almost any cost. Surely, goes the Jewish counter-argument, allowing lives to be lost would violate the tenets of Jewish ethics more so than bending any other principles would. Even were the law to take into account the dignity of the interrogation subject as *absolute*, might we not also be compelled to *suspend* this noble ideal in favor of finding out information to carry out the greater moral imperative of protecting innocent life?[11]

The sanctity of human life is the value with which Judaism is perhaps most preoccupied. Life—the tradition teaches—is *kinyan ha-kadosh baruch hu*, the property of God rather than of human beings, a principle whose practical implications include not only a prohibition against murder, but a prohibition against suicide and a refusal to allow murder to go unpunished.[12]

---

9. Justice Haim Cohn, *Katlan et al. v. The Prison Service et. al.* (1980), 34(3) *Piskei Din (Israeli Case Report)* 294 at 305–307. Cited and translated in Nahum Rakover, *Modern Applications of Jewish Law,* Library of Jewish Law, 1992, 199–202.
10. High Court of Justice 5100/94, *Public Committee Against Torture in Israel v. The State of Israel.* Full text is available at: http://www.jewishvirtuallibrary.org/jsource/Politics/GSStext.html.
11. See Michael Broyde, "Jewish Law and Torture," *Jewish Week* [July 7, 2006].
12. Maimonides, *Mishneh Torah, Hilkhot Rotzeah* 1:4

Jewish law recognizes not only a *right* to self-defense, but a positive *duty* to protect endangered life, elevating the "Good Samaritan" principle (that is, the duty to rescue) to the status of a legal requirement.[13] The law also commands that we hinder a perpetrator (*rodef;* lit. "pursuer") with force, even lethal force, from committing a crime, where no other means of prevention are available.

**Limits on Self-Defense**

Given the overwhelming sanctity of life, however, the Rabbis recognized the enormous danger of issuing an obligation that overrides the prohibition against force, and so they placed stringent limitations on applying the principle of defense:[14]

1. One must use *the minimum amount of necessary force to thwart a grave harm.* The Talmud teaches that if Person A

---

13. See Mishnah, *Sanhedrin* 8:7; Babylonian Talmud, *Sanhedrin* 73ff; *Shulchan Arukh, Hoshen Mishpat* 425:1–2. Rashi and Tosafot, ad. loc. *Sanhedrin* 73a; and Maimonides, *Mishneh Torah, Hilkhot Rotzeah* 1:6. As Chaim Povarsky elaborates, the principles of self-defense and defense of others (*rodef*) are related in later halakhic (Jewish legal) sources. For an extensive discussion of the relation between these two principles, see Povarsky's "The Law of the Pursuer and the Assassination of Prime Minister Rabin," *Jewish Law Association Studies IX*, E. A. Goodman, ed. (Binghamton, NY: Global Academic Publishing, 1997).
14. Some contemporary Jewish legal scholars argue that the *rodef* (lit. "pursuer") literature, with its stringent preconditions, applies only to conflicts within societies and not to wartime conditions. Generally, these arguments are made from silence. References to the *rodef* principle are not frequent in discussions of war—and commentators do not object when traditional texts describe war contexts that clearly violate *rodef* standards—so therefore the *rodef* preconditions must not apply to war. This essay applies these standards to the case of torture on three grounds: 1) several classical and contemporary traditional Jewish legal thinkers *do* explicitly apply these principles to battlefield contexts (E.g., Sifte Hachaim, 32:8, Immanuel Jakobovits, *Tradition: Journal of Orthodox Jewish Thought*, 4:2, 202, Shimon Weiser, "Purity of Arms: An Exchange of Letters," *Niv Hamidrashiyah* 11 (1974), 211–212). 2) Given the historical realities of the Jewish people during previous eras of Jewish history, there is a general paucity of halakhic treatment of war ethics issues, and no separate area of law governing *jus in bello* ("battlefield ethics") in *halakhah*. The most obvious place to turn in developing Judaism's positions on "battlefield ethics," is to general principles of self-defense, which closely resemble the ethical constraints of other *jus in bello* traditions. There is no reason to argue that these standards are *too* stringent when they are legitimately applied by other ethical systems and are the closest the Jewish system has to "rules of engagement." 3) The *rodef* principle is particularly germane to any discussion of torture, for the interrogation room lies closer to the courtroom than to the heat of the battlefield. Torture is often justified with criminal defenses, like the "necessity" defense, that resemble the *rodef* defense.

could have averted Person B's attack by maiming Person's B limb, rather than by killing him or her, then Person A is liable for Person B's death. In other words, one should shoot at another's feet before shooting at his or her chest.[15]

2. *Force must be a spontaneous reaction to present danger, not a premeditated act of preemption or revenge.* One may not kill or injure another to avenge or punish a crime. *Punishment* is reserved for the criminal justice system—with its careful inquiry into the facts, its procedural safeguards, and its presumption of innocence. One may cause harm in self-defense only in a moment of unavoidable urgency, when life is in immediate danger.[16]

3. One must be *reasonably certain* that a threat is real and that force is necessary to repel it. As in criminal law, this is an extremely difficult standard to apply. Nonetheless, this standard requires some minimal certainty in the evaluation of the threat and the likelihood that force will help avert it.[17]

Beyond rules concerning the general use of force, there are also guidelines as to the kind of tactics one may use in self-defense. Does torture as a tool of defense in an American military context meet the criteria of the following compelling standards?

1. *The minimum possible harm standard.* If military officers are supposed to cause enemies and suspected enemies "minimal possible harm," what would that look like in an interrogation room? Are there less harmful means than torture to protect public safety and innocent lives?

Research demonstrates that torture is ineffective, providing largely unreliable information, if not absolute fabrication, driven by both the victim's psychological instability while experiencing excruciating pain and

---

15. See Babylonian Talmud, *Sanhedrin* 74a and *Shulchan Arukh, Hoshen Mishpat* 421:13.
16. See for example, Maimonides, *Mishneh Torah, Hilkhot Geneiva* 9:7–10, Meir ben Baruch (Maharam bar Baruch) cited in Mordekhai, Bava Kamma 196, and Rashi, ad. loc., Exodus 22:1.
17. See for example, Maimonides, *Mishneh Torah, Hilkhot Rotzeah* 1:7, *Hilkhot Geneiva* 9:10, 9:12, Isaac ben Sheshet (Rivash), Responsa 238. See also *Mekhilta Nezikin* 13, 101 and Rashi and Ralbag ad loc. 22:2.

his or her belief that the torment will end if he or she tells a story—any story.[18] Furthermore, there are demonstrated, alternative ways of getting the information we need to protect lives. Interrogators report that rapport-building (winning over informants through earning their confidence) is the most effective method of interrogation, followed by non-violent ruses that catch suspects by surprise.[19] FBI documents claim that in Guantánamo, "every time the FBI established a rapport with a detainee, the military would step in and the detainee would stop being cooperative."[20]

Physical coercion is neither the least harmful nor the most effective means of obtaining the information we need to protect ourselves. Given that there is little demonstrated proof that torture "works," and that effective alternative means are available to gather intelligence necessary to protect American lives, torture would not seem to be permissible according to a "minimum possible harm" standard.

2. *The principle of imminent danger.* The use of "torture lite" in American detention facilities in cases where interrogators were not fighting against an imminent attack has been well-documented. U.S. military personnel have used physically coercive techniques not only to deactivate "ticking bombs," where lives were in immediate danger, but also to obtain information about who was involved in previous attacks, to learn who is generally hostile to American policies, to punish, intimidate, and pacify detainees, and to send a message to detainees' families and communities.

Jewish law requires that *violence* be used in self-defense only as an expression of unavoidable urgency, when life is in immediate peril. Such a standard would allow the killing of a suicide bomber strapped with explosives, or the return of enemy fire in battle. It would *not* permit *deliberate, routine, premeditated violence* in the calculated conditions of the interrogation room, in which a subject poses no imminent threat and is at the interrogator's mercy.

But what about a true "ticking bomb" case, one might ask? The "ticking bomb" presents some version of the following hypothetical: A captured

---

18. John Conroy, *Unspeakable Acts, Ordinary People: The Dynamics of Torture* (Berkeley, CA: University of California Press, 2001), 113, 170.
19. Jane Mayer, "Whatever It Takes," *The New Yorker,* Feb. 19, 2007.
20. Quoted in Anne Applebaum's editorial, "The Torture Myth," *Washington Post,* Jan. 12, 2005, A21, at http://www.washingtonpost.com/wp-dyn/articles/A2302-2005Jan11.html. Cf. Joseph Lelyveld, "Interrogating Ourselves," *New York Times Magazine,* June 12, 2005 and Conroy, *Unspeakable Acts, Ordinary People,* 44.

fanatic has hidden an explosive in the heart of a major metropolis, set to go off within hours. The authorities are certain that the prisoner in their hands is the perpetrator, whose knowledge could forestall the catastrophe and spare thousands of innocents, but the non-violent devices of their most expert interrogators have not yielded enough information to locate and disable the bomb.

The problem with the "ticking bomb" case is that it seems not to have occurred in the real world. It is an implausible hypothetical that relies on several dubious preconditions: you know an attack is due to occur imminently, that the person you are interrogating harbors the information that could prevent the attack, and that he or she will reveal reliable information once subjected to pain, etc.

These circumstances are unlikely even within the realm of the thought experiment in which they seem exclusively to reside. For how certain does one have to be that the party being interrogated knows something? May one utilize torture based on mere suspicion? Why not torture hundreds, if not thousands, in a context like Iraq, in which everyone is a potential enemy, in which everyone may know *something*, and where there are always bombs primed to explode—if not in an hour, then tomorrow, or next week?

On the empirical, historical level, in Algeria, during the French occupation, in Israel and the Occupied Territories, and recently in Iraq and Afghanistan, defense of torture under "ticking bomb" conditions has invariably opened the door to the *normalization* of torture. Whenever advanced preparation and legal authorization for "the ticking bomb" exception has occurred, torture has become entrenched as an administrative practice and a customary procedure for interrogation and governance. Thus, it was not used in isolated circumstances in which harsh treatment was heroically employed to fend off catastrophe, but rather it became an ongoing and somewhat indiscriminate regime of cruel and dehumanizing treatment.

The "ticking bomb" scenario is an artificial philosopher's case that cannot withstand exposure to real world conditions. As NYU Law Professor Aziz Huq has said, "Laws must comport to the world in which we live, not the world with which the Fox channel presents us. It is morally fraudulent to make law on the basis of infidelity to reality."[21]

---

21. Public Lecture, "When Does Prosecution Become Persecution? Torture: Is it Ever Moral?" Jan. 25, 2007.

It is not only *fraudulent*, but *dangerous* to use this case as a guide for moral and legal reflection about torture in the real world.

3. *The certainty standard.* This principle is difficult to apply in a barroom brawl, let alone in a world in which shadowy "threats" are pervasive, ongoing and unpredictable. In our struggle to protect the public from terror, how do we ascertain the degree of actual versus perceived threat, and what kind or degree of force will contribute to ameliorating said threats, rather than exacerbating them?

These may seem like tactical questions, but as Jewish law recognizes, it is impossible to disentangle moral questions from the practical, empirical, and even political situations in which they arise.

Consider the following: In 1995, a man named Yigal Amir assassinated Yitzhak Rabin, the Prime Minister of Israel, on the grounds that he was a *rodef* ("pursuer") threatening massive loss of life. He argued that Rabin, in pursuing a path of territorial accommodation with Palestinians, was endangering the survival not only of the State of Israel, but also of the entire Jewish people. In the end, one ground for the rejection of Amir's reasoning was *uncertainty*.[22] After all, at least half of the Israeli voting public believed that terminating the peace process would be at least as dangerous as continuing it. Thus, if no one could be certain that Rabin was an immediate threat, then Amir certainly had no defensible rationale for killing him.

## The Dangers of Torture

In closing, I will delineate four reasons why torturing detainees is *at least* as dangerous to the American people as refraining from doing so.

1. *Even if torture helps win a battle, it typically helps lose the larger war.*[23] In the aftermath of Abu Ghraib, bipartisan military and political commentators recognized that America had granted Osama bin Laden his most effective propaganda campaign and recruitment tool yet.[24] Even if torturing detainees helps garner "actionable intelligence"

---

22. See for example, Povarsky, "The Law of the Pursuer and the Assassination of Prime Minister Rabin," 180.
23. Michael Ignatieff, *The Lesser Evil: Political Ethics in an Age of Terror* (Princeton, NJ: Princeton University Press, 2004), 19–20.
24. See Phillip Carter, "The Road to Abu Ghraib," *Washington Monthly,* November 2004. Available at www.washingtonmonthly.com/features/2004/0411.carter.html; Bob Herbert, "It Just Gets Worse," *New York Times,* July 11, 2005.

on terror networks, what good is a military tactic that helps break a terror cell while alienating both allies and moderates and engendering hatred and resentment in an entire population?[25]

Thomas Friedman has been particularly eloquent on this point:

> I am convinced that more Americans are dying and will die if we keep the Gitmo prison open than if we shut it down … This is not just deeply immoral, it is strategically dangerous … I would rather have a few more bad guys roaming the world than a whole new generation.[26]

We will not ultimately help the American people to live in greater security by fanning existing hostilities and bolstering the idea that America is an "evil occupier" intent on brutalizing and dehumanizing Muslims under our jurisdiction.

2. *Torture erodes America's global political legitimacy and credibility.* Perhaps nothing has done more to undermine America's standing in the world than the torture scandals that began with Abu Ghraib in 2004, as well the total impunity of those public officials who should have been held accountable for them.[27]

3. *Torture endangers our own soldiers,* undermining longstanding international protections against the mistreatment of POWs and dismantling our ability to oppose similar practices when they are used against American citizens.[28]

4. *Torture threatens American ideals—everything we stand for—the only real counteragent to terror.*

---

25. Ignatieff, *The Lesser Evil,* 82; Walzer, *Arguing About War* (New Haven, CT: Yale University Press, 2004), 9.
26. "Just Shut it Down," *New York Times,* May 27, 2005.
27. See Samantha Power, "Fixing Foreign Policy," *Harvard Magazine,* July–Aug. 2006.
28. Former Secretary of State Colin Powell's criticism of the Bybee memo—which argued for the elimination of Geneva protections in Guantánamo and Afghanistan—is available at http://msnbc.msn.com/id/4999363/site/newsweek. Powell claims: "[The Bybee memo] will reverse over a century of U.S. policy and practice in supporting the Geneva Conventions and undermine the protections of the law of war for our troops, both in this specific context and in general." See also the critical memo of William H. Taft, IV, legal advisor to the State Department, at http://www.fas.org/sgp/othergov/taft.pdf. For an expanded version of this argument, cf. Carter, "The Road to Abu Ghraib."

The sanctity of human personhood lies at the core of Judaism, and also is the foundation of our history as a nation. The repudiation of the rack and the screw and the institution of due process protections were seen by our constitutional forefathers as the foundation for the modern rule of law, an enlightened bulwark against persecution and tyranny, and essential for dignity, liberty, security, and well-being. The Supreme Court has long denounced physical and psychological cruelty on the part of governmental agents as "revolting," "shocking," and "alien" to America's most sacred values.[29]

Let us heed the historian's warning: democracies are defeated by terrorism not in military conflict, but in the erosion of their ideals through overreaction.[30] To paraphrase legal scholar Lisa Hajjar, if America sacrifices the one right that is considered most sacrosanct and inalienable by U.S. and international law, the one right the civilized world agrees all human beings should have simply by virtue of being human—dignity—not only the "terrorists" will lose. All human beings will lose.[31]

---

29. See for example, *Culombe v. Connecticut* 367 U.S. at 581 (1961) for a summary of "[a] cluster of convictions, each expressive in a different manifestation of the basic notion that the terrible engine of the criminal law is not to be used to overreach individuals who stand helpless against it. Among these are the notions that men are not to be imprisoned at the unfettered will of their prosecutors, nor subjected to physical brutality by the officials charged with the investigation of crime. This principle, branded into the consciousness of our civilization by the memory of the secret inquisitions, sometimes practiced with torture, which were borrowed briefly from the continent during the era of the Star Chamber, was well known to those who established the American government."
30. Ignatieff, *The Lesser Evil,* 61.
31. "Hajjar, "Torture and the Future," *Middle East Report Online,* May 2004.

# CASE 4

# NATIONAL POLICIES CONCERNING WAR

## Case Study

### A. The Military-Industrial Complex

"In the councils of government, we must guard against the acquisition of unwarranted influence, whether sought or unsought, by the military-industrial complex. The potential for the disastrous rise of misplaced power exists and will persist." So spoke then-President Dwight D. Eisenhower in 1961.

Does the military feed on itself? Is the U.S. economy dependent on our military system? Is the U.S. dependent on war as a way of maintaining its place in the world? Does the military-industrial complex create incentives to wage war?

### B. The Military Draft

Since the United States ended the military draft in 1973, all American military activities have been carried out by a volunteer army. Should the draft be reinstituted?

Historically, soldiers have primarily come from lower socio-economic classes, though recent evidence suggests an increasing number come from the middle class. The military provides financial incentives to attract enrollment and reenlistment in the armed forces, which is especially critical since people can no longer be required to service through conscription. What moral issues does it raise to tie service in the armed forces to monetary benefits? Would reinstituting the draft serve to distribute the responsibility for service more or less fairly among Americans of different class backgrounds?

### C. Military Spending

Engaging in war inevitably results in allocating a high percentage of a nation's resources to military spending, often resulting in the devotion of a much lower percentage to domestic needs (e.g., infrastructure, education, welfare, health care, cultural initiatives, etc.) Should this be a deterrent to entering war? Should it be a reason to try to end a war? Is military spending too high in proportion to spending on other priorities in times of relative peace? How do you weigh national security against domestic needs in today's world?

## D. Arms Trading

Both the United States and Israel do a considerable amount of research to develop new weapons, and often sell some of those weapons to other countries for a large profit. Are there any moral problems with this? Does it matter where the weapons go? What should be the criteria for determining who is an acceptable buyer? Does it matter who makes money from these sales? What if weapons (including nuclear weapons) are sold for a guarantee that the purchasing country will not develop weapons of its own?

## Traditional Sources

*Compiled by Uzi Weingarten and the Editors*

### The Military Draft

**1. Numbers 31:4**

You shall dispatch on the campaign a thousand from every one of the tribes of Israel.

**2. Numbers 32:6**

Moses replied to the Gadites and the Reubenites, "Are your brothers to go to war [to conquer Canaan on the west bank of the Jordan River] while you stay here [on the eastern bank of the Jordan River]?"

**3. Deuteronomy 20:1–7**

When you take the field against your enemies, and see horses and chariots—forces larger than yours—have no fear of them, for the Lord your God, who brought you from the land of Egypt, is with you. Before you join battle, the priest shall come forward and address the troops. He shall say to them, "Hear, O Israel! You are about to join battle with your enemy. Let not your courage falter. Do not be in fear, or in panic, or in dread of them. For it is the Lord your God who marches with you to do battle for you against your enemy, to bring you to victory."

Then the officials shall address the troops, as follows: "Is there anyone who has built a new house but has not dedicated it? Let him go back to his home, lest he die in battle and another dedicate it. Is there anyone who has planted a vineyard but has never harvested it? Let him go back to his home, lest he die in battle and another harvest it. Is there anyone who has paid the bride-price for a wife, but who has not yet married her? Let him go back to his home, lest he die in battle and another marry her."

**a. Rashi, commentary on verse 5:**

[The builder, planter, and new groom are sent back because] it is a matter of [preventing] anguish.

### b. Abraham Ibn Ezra (1089–1164, Spain and North Africa), commentary to verse 5:

The reason is that his thought and all his desire are to dedicate his house, and therefore he will flee and cause others to flee [in his wake].

## 4. Deuteronomy 20:8

The officials shall go on addressing the troops and say, "Is there anyone afraid and disheartened? Let him go back to his home, lest the courage of his comrades flag like his."

### a. Abraham Ibn Ezra's commentary on this verse:

"Afraid" to strike another; "faint of heart" and [unable] to endure being struck.

### b. Maimonides (Rambam), *Mishneh Torah*, Laws of Kings and Wars 7:15

"Who is afraid and faint of heart" [should be read according to] its literal meaning, that he does not have the courage to withstand the thick of battle. Once he enters the thick of battle, he should rely on Israel's Hope and its Rescuer in times of distress … and risk his life, and not fear or be afraid, and not think about his wife or his children, but erase their memory from his heart, and turn away from everything [and focus on] the war. And whoever begins to think and to doubt during the war and frightens himself violates a negative commandment, as it is written (Deuteronomy 20:3): "Let your hearts not be faint, do not fear and do not quake and do not be terrified." If he did not triumph and did not wage war with all his heart and soul, it is as if he shed everybody's blood, as it is written (Deuteronomy 20:8): "So that he not melt the heart of his brethren as his own heart."

## 5. Mishnah, *Sotah* 8:7

To what does this [the exemptions from service] apply? To discretionary wars [*milhamot reshut*], but in wars commanded by the Torah [*milhamot mitzvah*] all go forth, even a bridegroom from his chamber and a bride from her canopy. Rabbi Judah says: To what extent do these verses apply? To wars commanded by the Torah [*milhamot mitzvah*], but in obligatory wars [*milhamot hovah*] all go forth, even a bridegroom from his chamber and a bride from her canopy.

### 6. Maimonides, *Mishneh Torah*, Laws of Kings and Wars 7:9, 10, 11

[9] All those [who fought and] who return from the front … provide water and food to their brethren in the army, and fix the roads.

[10] But those who do not go to battle at all are not obliged to do anything [for the war effort]—namely, one who builds a house and dedicated it [that is, entered it to live in it for the first time], and one who marries his fiancée … or began to eat the fruits of his vineyard [in the fourth year, when he is first permitted to eat them but only in Jerusalem, in fulfillment of Lev. 19:24] shall not go to battle until the end of the year, as the Torah says, "He shall be free for his house for one year, and bring joy to his wife whom he has taken" (Deuteronomy 24:5) … From the Oral Tradition we learn: He shall be free one year whether for the house he has built, or the woman he married, or the vineyard whose fruits he began to eat. [He need not have done all three to qualify for the exemption but only one of them.]

[11] That entire year he does not provide water and food [to the troops] or fix the roads, and does not guard at the city wall … as it is written (Deuteronomy 24:5): "He shall not go out in the army and shall not cross over on its account for any matter." [The two prohibitions of not going out and not crossing over refer] one to the [defensive] needs of the city and the other to the needs of the battalion.

## Domestic Policy and War

### 7. Maimonides, *Mishneh Torah*, Laws of Kings and Wars 4:10

In all matters, [the king's] actions should be for the sake of heaven, and his purpose and thought should be to raise the true Law (i.e., the Torah), and to fill the world with justice, and to break the might of the wicked, and to fight God's wars. For a king is placed on the throne only for the purpose of doing justice and [fighting] wars, as it is written (1 Samuel 18:20): "And our king shall adjudicate [between] us, and fight our wars."

### 8. Rashi to Deuteronomy 20:1

If you do equitable justice, you are promised that if you go to war you are victorious. And similarly David says (Psalms 119:121): "I have done equitable justice, do not leave me to my oppressors."

## Arms Trading

### 9. Isaiah 2:3–4

> For instruction shall come forth from Zion,
> The word of the Lord from Jerusalem.
> Thus He will judge among the nations
> And arbitrate for the many peoples,
> And they shall beat their swords into plowshares
> And their spears into pruning hooks:
> Nation shall not take up
> Sword against nation;
> They shall never again know war.

### 10. Joel 4:9–10, 13

> Proclaim this among the nations:
> Prepare for battle!
> Arouse the warriors,
> Let all the fighters come and draw near!
> Beat your plowshares into swords,
> And your pruning hooks into spears.
> Let even the weakling say, "I am strong."…
> Swing the sickle,
> For the crop is ripe;
> Come and tread,
> For the winepress is full,
> The vats are overflowing!
> For great is their wickedness.

# Contemporary Sources

*Compiled by Steven Edelman-Blank*

## The Military Draft

**1. Immanuel Jakobovits, "The Morality of Warfare, United Synagogue Lecture, 25 May 1982, Central Synagogue, London" in *Jewish Preaching in Times of War 1800–2001*, Marc Saperstein, ed. (Oxford: The Littman Library of Jewish Civilization, 2008), 525**

Among the biblical rules of conscription, exemption from army service is granted to betrothed and newly-wed men (Deut. 20:7, 24:5). The express reason given for this exemption is that the newly-married man "shall be free for his house one year, and he shall rejoice his wife whom he has taken" (Deut. 24:5). To rejoice one's wife is regarded as a full-time occupation, especially during the first year of marriage, which often either makes or breaks the marriage.

This duty is considered as a national and not just a personal obligation. By consolidating your marriage, this law teaches, you perform a greater service to your nation, to the survival of your people, by having a stable home than by joining the army and defending the people in military battle. The ultimate security of our people lies in our homes. Had we relied merely on military strength and victories, we would have been extinct long ago. Hence, in the choice to be made here between home and army, priority was to be given to the home. By staying home for the first year "to rejoice your wife" you render a more essential service to the nation than by joining its defenders in the trenches. In the moral scale of values, then, even in terms of Jewish security, happy homes come before powerful armies. Jewish homes are our principal fortifications, our first line of national defence[sic].

2. **Reuven Kimelman, "The Ethics of National Power: Government and War from the Sources of Judaism,"** *Perspectives* **[February 1987], 16–17**

Besides having to be substantiated, the economic and familial exemptions share another common denominator. Projects such as starting a house, beginning a vineyard, or getting engaged mostly affect men in their prime, which is precisely the age of maximum combat readiness. A large number of exemptions for this age group can so hamper mobilization efforts as to impair the military effort …

There is a loophole in the war legislation. A loophole so gaping that it allows those not convinced of the validity of the war to reassert their sovereignty through legal shenanigans. Doubts about the validity of the war will stir up their own social momentum and induce many to seek wholesale exemptions. The result is a war declared by the executive and approved by the Sanhedrin which sputters for failing to persuade the populace of its necessity.

Mobilization cannot succeed without a high degree of popular motivation. Many will express their half-heartedness by dragging their feet in the hope of being, as the Talmud says, "The last to go to war and the first to return." Through expressing their reluctance to fight, the populace retains a semblance of sovereignty and indirectly passes judgment on whether the military venture is both necessary and serves legitimate political ends.

3. **Matthew Moosey, "'A Family Tradition' Campus Diaries," *New Voices: National Jewish Student Magazine* (February 21, 2002). Available at http://www.newvoices.org/campus?id=0071**

Judaism is very clear on the importance of service. Hillel said that the greatest commandment and the essence of all Torah was to love your neighbor as yourself. I consider military service the right way for me to do this. I can certainly say that being Jewish inspired me all the more to take on the challenge of military service.

4. **Jonathan Nitzan and Shimshon Bichler, "Cheap Wars," *Tikkun* (March 27, 2007)**

The idea of a mass, "voluntary" army was born out of the French Revolution. The new soldiers turned out to be cheaper and more loyal than mercenaries, and they fought well. However, the masses needed to be educated so that they could read the newspapers and follow the propaganda—hence the birth of compulsory "elementary" schooling. Later on, the proles started to demand additional perks. They wanted culture, insurance, pensions and veteran benefits. In the 1910s, the elites cheated them. They sent the masses to be butchered by the millions in the trenches of World War I, and then abandoned those who returned as veterans. This experience raised the ante. In the early 1940s, the citizen-soldiers had to be offered a whole welfare state, so that they would be willing to get butchered, again, in the Second World War. What initially looked like "soldiers for free" turned out to be a rather expensive way of fighting wars.

The last expensive war was Vietnam. With neoliberal globalization replacing the welfare-warfare state, there was no longer a need for mass armies with high overhead. Instead, the capitalists started to invest in "smart weapons" that could be operated by high-school dropouts and cause plenty of damage. They abandoned the draft in favor of purely professional armies—partly governmental, partly private.

A similar process has taken place in Israel.

5. **Stuart A. Cohen, "Dilemmas of Military Service in Israel: The Religious Dimension" in *War and Peace in the Jewish Tradition*, Lawrence Schiffman and Joel B. Wolowelsky, eds. (New York: Yeshiva University Press, 2007). The Orthodox Forum Series, Series Editor, Robert S. Hirt, 330–331**

The monopolistic claims of *Torah* study—especially vis-à-vis military service—have found their most explicit expression in *haredi* circles. It is now calculated that over 80% of *haredi* males of conscript age presently claim—and receive—extensive deferments from enlistment on the grounds that "the [study of] the *Torah* is their profession" (*Toratam umanutam*). Indeed, this particular segment of Orthodox Israeli society now posits as an article of faith the argument that the energies that its members invest in their scholarly vocation contribute as much (if not more) to Israel's ultimate survival than do the exertions of IDF troops.

## Technology and the Arms Race

6. **"Arms Control," Religious Action Center of Reform Judaism. Available at http://rac.org/advocacy/issues/issueac/**

The collapse of the Soviet Union and the end of the nuclear arms race between the United States and the U.S.S.R. has created a vastly different global environment, one that requires new concepts of peace and security. However, the United States continues to spend an outrageous amount of money annually to maintain and improve its military apparatus. As leader of the free world and outspoken advocate of arms control and reduction, the United States' record on non-proliferation is both surprising and alarming.

7. **"Statement Of Rabbi Amy Klein, Director Of Congregational Relations, Religious Action Center Of Reform Judaism International Campaign To Ban Landmines Rally," May 16, 1997, Religious Action Center of Reform Judaism. Available at http://rac.org/Articles/index.cfm?id=621&pge_prg_id=4237**

A year ago, we celebrated the President's affirmation of support for the international campaign to ban all anti-personnel landmines, and we were filled with hope that American leadership would bring a speedy end to the deaths caused by these deadly weapons …

Next year at this time, may we be harvesting grain—not sowing the soil with the blood of the innocent. Let us pray today that we cease using the earth as a destroyer of life. Let us sow the soil with seed—not with mines—so that "the earth will sprout vegetation: seedbearing plants, fruit trees of every kind …" Let us go forth and plant in the land that it will give sustenance to our children rather than take their lives.

8. **"Boost in U.S. Aid to Israel Vital Amid Increasing Threats," The American Israel Public Affairs Committee. Available at http://www.aipac.org/The_Issues/index_11073.asp**

The U.S.-Israel alliance remains more critical than ever as the two countries face an unprecedented array of shared threats. From a potential nuclear-armed Iran to the expanding military capabilities of the terrorist groups Hamas and Hizballah, Israel is finding it increasingly difficult—and expensive—to meet these challenges. Implementation of a 2007 U.S.-Israeli security agreement, which pledges to provide Israel with $30 billion in military assistance during the next decade, is vital to ensuring that Israel maintains its qualitative military edge over those adversaries that threaten the Jewish state and actively work to undermine U.S. interests in the region.

9. *The Seventh Day: Soldiers Talk about the Six-Day War*, **Avraham Shapira and Henry Near, eds. (New York: Charles Scribner's Sons, 1970), 146, 148**

*Amos:* But can you live that way forever—with the feeling that every few years we're going to find ourselves with our backs against the wall? With the feeling that every few years foreigners are going to be intent on killing you? Can you imagine living this way and still being the same person, the same nation in a few years' time? Can it be done without our getting to the stage in which we'll quite simply hate them? Just hate them. I don't mean that we'll take delight in killing, or turn into sadists. Simply deep bitter hatred for them for having forced such a life on us …

*Nachman:* … Here we are asking ourselves, nagging at ourselves again and again, worrying about what effects it will have on us. What scars will it leave? How are we going to educate the youth? Won't they all be very militaristic? But what else can you suggest?

10. **Roland B. Gittelsohn, "The Birth of a New Freedom, 14 March 1945, U.S. Marine Corps Cemetery, Iwo Jima" in *Jewish Preaching in Times of War 1800–2001*, Marc Saperstein, ed. (Oxford: The Littman Library of Jewish Civilization, 2008), 484–485**

When the final cross has been placed in the last cemetery, once again there will be those to whom profit is more important than peace, who will insist with the voice of sweet reasonableness and appeasement that it is better to trade with the enemies of mankind than, by crushing them, to lose their profit. To you who sleep here silently, we give our promise: we will not listen! We will not forget that some of you were burnt with oil that came from American wells, that many of you were killed with shells fashioned from American steel. We promise that when once again men seek profit at your expense, we shall remember how you looked when you were placed reverently, lovingly, in the ground.

# Responses

## A Solemn Duty: Citizens' Responsibilities for the Nation's Wars and Warriors

Harold L. Robinson

THE NATION President Eisenhower addressed in 1961, when he first described the "military-industrial complex," had a vastly different cultural attitude toward the military than that which we have today. Nineteen million Americans had recently served in World War Two (WWII) at a time when the nation's total population barely exceeded 150 million. Even those who had not served in the military made enormous sacrifices to assist in the war effort. Consumer goods were rationed or unavailable altogether. School children gathered scrap metal to be converted into jeeps and other equipment, paper to be used for packing materials, and used clothing, to be made into uniforms. Consequently, WWII gave many Americans a familiarity with and emotional investment in the military, as well as a profound appreciation for our national sacrifices and military successes. By 1961, WWII veterans were only 35- to 50-years old, and the ranks of veterans had been swollen by many who served in Korea and those conscripted through the peace-time draft.

When Eisenhower spoke, most Americans viewed the world through its conflict with The Soviet Union. The so-called "Cold War" and the specter of thermo-nuclear war were ever present. Some suburban homes had fallout shelters, and many public buildings and schools had special emergency supplies so that they could serve the surviving population if a nuclear exchange occurred. Even in the relative peace of 1961, our nation of 180 million supported an armed force of 3.5 million active duty personnel, but that constituted only about 2% of the nation's population. Soldiers were stationed around the world, from Germany to Turkey in Europe, and from Korea to the Straits of Formosa off the coast of China in Asia.

Thus, former General Eisenhower's address as President was made to a nation that lacked a healthy skepticism of the military. As one of the leading military figures of WWII, Eisenhower was perfectly positioned to issue a cautionary statement. However, his warning against the military-industrial complex was only one note in a larger refrain. In that same speech he warned against excessive government funding of scientific research and the rise of a scientific-technological elite made up of scientists, engineers, physicians, architects, industrialists, and others privy to the inner workings of government and industry, but involved in projects little understood by those outside their fields. Thus, Eisenhower was concerned that such an elite could gain power and influence over large segments of our national life. Most prophetically, though, he warned Americans about "the impulse to live only for today, plundering ... the precious resources of tomorrow."

**The American Military and Economy Today**
America is a very different country almost a half-century after Eisenhower's speech. Today less than 5% of Congress members have served in the military. Our active duty forces number less than 1.5 million out of 300 million, which equals less than half of one percent of the nation's populace. Today, there is also no draft. When the draft existed, many received a deferment to attend college before their military service. Thus, it was not uncommon for Jewish professionals to have served in the military after getting the necessary educational qualifications, prior to entering civilian life and starting their practices. Yet today, only an estimated 10,000 Jews serve in our nation's armed forces, on either active or reserve duty.

America has twice gone to war recently without expecting significant sacrifice on the home front. President Lyndon Johnson made a similar mistake when he sought to fight the War on Poverty at home even as America fought in Vietnam. I wonder how much of the devastating inflation of the 1970s can be attributed to the attempt to fight a war abroad without a parallel call to economic sacrifice at home. In the 2000s, we have expended vast treasure on the War in Iraq without limiting the expansion of the consumer economy at home. So, too, I wonder how much of today's economic nightmare is a penalty for the government's delinquency in paying the 700 trillion dollars spent so far in Iraq back to the national budget. Our nation has fought two of our most recent major conflicts, those in Iraq and Afghanistan, without openly acknowledging both the wars' costs and the resulting necessity for diminished domestic spending. Thus, the domestic cost of war has hardly been a deterrent to entering conflicts, but it has become a huge impediment to military success.

It is for economic reasons that I therefore question the underlying premises of the case study and its attendant questions. Our service economy is far less enmeshed in military production today than the manufacturing economy was in 1961. Military contracts seem lucrative for some local economies where there are defense plants, but their value to the national economy is questionable. Military production is not part of a larger economic cycle. Consumer products are purchased by customers, as part of a vast economic system, while military production is purchased by the national treasury with money siphoned out of the system through taxes. Thus, rather than sustaining the economy, military spending drains the economy, while war drains our resources even more dramatically.

This raises two moral questions: What responsibility do citizens have to openly and willingly assume the cost of armed conflict through increased taxes and the resulting decreased consumption? What are the moral ramifications of sending our volunteer force to fight a war that we, if called upon, would be unwilling to fight ourselves?

**The Responsibilities of Citizens**

Because America has standing armed forces, it has forces in waiting. This creates the ability to enter into conflicts without demanding a high level of commitment from the nation. However, sustaining such efforts requires additional personnel through the mobilization of reserves (Iraq) or a draft (Vietnam). Consequently, without the widely held commitment of individual citizens to the cause being fought, which creates a popular consensus, sustaining a military campaign becomes difficult and often fails. Such was the case in Vietnam and, I believe, in Iraq.

Nations engage in war either in response to an attack or as the result of a decision by their leaders. In democracies, such decisions must be made by democratically elected officials, such as our President and members of Congress. However, our history teaches us that we are most likely to succeed in a war when the decision-making institutions these leaders are a part of reflect a consensus among Americans about the just and important nature of that war. In a democracy, such a consensus usually requires an open debate among elements of a well-informed body politic. When these elements are lacking, the will to sustain a military effort often collapses.

I believe that a more knowledgeable and well-informed citizenry that possesses a healthy skepticism of those leaders calling us to arms, and that is more directly linked to the personal and economic costs of conflict, might prevent the needless use of military force in the future. At the same time, citizens can empower our military to act on those rare but extraordinarily vital occasions when force is truly needed to defend ourselves or others. I wonder how many unnecessary conflicts could be avoided and how many lives could be saved if every war authorization by Congress automatically triggered a broad-based draft of citizens for both the armed forces and other forms of national service, and also called for a substantial war tax that would force citizens to bear the expense of the war and, as a result, would limit consumer consumption. Both would make Americans realize the true costs of conflict.

## The Duties of Soldiers and Our Duties to Them

Chaplains are empowered to explore the innermost feelings of usually stoic service members in ways other members of the military simply can't. As a chaplain in the U.S. military for 36 years, I have been privileged to be the confidant of service members from the most junior recruit in boot camp to very senior generals and admirals in positions of high responsibility. Part of what I have discovered from these experiences is that while a vast range of perspectives on the ethics and justice of specific wars and policies exists within the military, virtually all individual troops think about in combat is the immediate mission confronting them and its impact on their buddies—the people who depend on them and on whom they depend.

During the worst years of Operation Iraqi Freedom, junior soldiers' questions about the military-industrial complex were as simple as, "Where can I find enough scrap metal to provide armor for my soft-shelled Humvee or truck?" or, "Why am I buying my own body armor when it should be supplied by the Army or Marine Corps?" In short, they never questioned the justice of the war or even of their mission, but they challenged the injustice of being sent to war without adequate resources for themselves and their buddies.

More senior officers added to these questions. One lieutenant colonel who had been in Afghanistan in 2003 and again in 2006 asked me rhetorically, "Why won't they give us the resources to make a difference here? These people [Afghans] trusted us, and we promised them we would help them create a whole village. It would not cost a lot, but all of our resources have dried up or have gone to OIF [Operation Iraqi Freedom] and we are failing them." Around the same time, a three-star general commented, after a tour in Iraq, "We were told not to worry about what to do after regime change in Iraq—DOD [Department of Defense] and DOS [Department of State] would be there for us to carry on the mission after Saddam fell. So we decapitated the regime and turned around to hand off the baton, but there was no one there but us." A four-star general also told me that he was offered a major command job, which was a huge promotion, but that he accepted only on the condition that the requirements placed on his soldiers would not "break the force," rendering them ineffective and incapable, unable to fulfill their primary mission. Just like the junior combat soldiers, this general was watching out for his folks, the ones who depended on him and on whom he relied.

The point is that soldiers, sailors, airmen, and marines at all levels worry more about the justice of what is happening to them in the field of combat than about the justice of the war itself. When asked about the war in Iraq, each individual soldier holds his or her personal opinion to him or herself, reciting the mantra, "That's for our civilian masters to decide." Many have surprised me with the same sentence, quoting the epitaph to the Spartan dead at Thermopylae:

> Go tell the Spartans, thou who passest by,
> That here, obedient to their laws, we lie.

To be sure, our service men and women generally believe they are doing the right thing, a good and noble thing of which they are immensely proud. They believe that their mission is just because our country's political leadership, which represents the nation as a whole, has set them upon it. Therefore, we all have a great responsibility to participate in the decision to go to war and to send our forces into harm's way. As such, I agree with President Eisenhower that we must require our government to guard against the influence of the military-industrial complex as it pertains to launching military action.

## War, Peace, and National Security: A Theme and Variations

Linda B. Miller

READING PRESIDENT Dwight D. Eisenhower's dire warnings from 1961 about the military-industrial complex and the dangers of "misplaced power" now invites personal recollections of a life spent teaching and doing research on "national security."

In the decades since Ike spoke these words, they have been parsed endlessly. Nevertheless, a key issue he highlighted—the general connection between foreign policy and domestic politics—has sometimes faded into the background as other, more specific questions on arms races or the military draft have gained prominence.

This case study on national policies concerning war allows us to place Ike's caution in a larger, present-day context, when the tensions between the two spheres of government activity, international and national, seem especially fraught. Once again, a president who wishes to enact sweeping domestic legislation must deal with a host of international challenges.

Not surprisingly, President Barack Obama is being compared not only to his favorite previous presidents, Abraham Lincoln and George Washington, but also to Lyndon Johnson, who wanted passage of the Great Society legislation domestically but was crippled by the Vietnam War. Is the health care–Afghanistan equation similar? Since resources are finite, choices must be made between competing priorities. When military conflict is occurring, those choices are much more constrained. Ike's anxieties thus seem prescient and wise. His remarks were widely quoted, but later were often taken out of context. In fact, as I recall, in 1961, they were noted favorably but rarely analyzed in depth.

When Ike delivered his speech, I was a graduate student in political science at Columbia, where he had served as president after his military career ended. I planned to enter government service rather than stay in academe, and I was eager to enter this essentially male-dominated field. As I continued my rush toward graduation and entering the so-called real world, I had no idea that such comments were so far-sighted or that my own research decades later would build on Ike's insights. Indeed, the study of national security in U.S. think tanks and academic settings would proceed for years along familiar lines, stressing

Cold War imperatives, the American success story, and the possibilities of nuclear war.

**Theory and Practice**

After the fall of the Berlin Wall, and even more forcefully after the collapse of the Soviet Empire, worries about Ike's concerns mounted. The U.S. academic establishment (or at least the Ivy League institutions where I was advancing my career) was slow to move its focus away from the Cold War, which had assumed primacy in traditional national security discussions. But eventually, when foundations began grant-making activities that broadened the scope of acceptable research agendas to include investigating the connections between national security and domestic politics, the academic community followed the money.

A few years later, the study of ethics in international affairs, once considered a marginal topic at best, gained recognition as younger scholars explored religious traditions. Could these traditions yield any guidance for the perplexed social scientists intellectually stranded after the end of the Cold War? Could some classical texts of Judaism, for example, tell us anything about war and peace that would be relevant in the "new" post-Cold War international politics, when American advantages in military power were of perhaps less consequence in securing U.S. goals than they had been for the previous half century? Clearly, these are still important questions to pose, and there are still a variety of answers to them.

Just as generals are often accused of planning for previous wars, so too, many theorists and policymakers suffer from the same tendency, dictating the political agenda and government spending. Understandably, observers or political leaders who lived through World War II and the struggle against the "isms" of that time—Nazism in Germany and Communism in the Soviet Union—elevated foreign policy imperatives over domestic priorities like education and health care, the very issues that are so prominent today in U.S. domestic politics.

This enduring contest between foreign policy requirements and domestic demands for both resources and priority is what stirred Eisenhower to issue his caveat in 1961. That contest is ongoing, and so we should consider it to be a structural problem in American politics. What Ike understood from his years in the military and then in politics was that there was a price to be paid for the insistence that the U.S.

must prevail in the struggle with Communism, even if that meant that "the military-industrial complex" gained influence over Congress, the White House, and perhaps even the courts. That price would be the diminution of the checks and balances that are at the core of American democracy. In the early 21$^{st}$ century, it is the recent substitution of "terrorism" for "Communism" that should concern us in reference to Ike's words.

**Progress**

Where are we today? I think we are in a better place. First, the inherent tension between rival demands in the foreign and domestic realms is better understood, ironically, even as the line between what is "foreign" and what is "domestic" has eroded. Second, the new media, while problematic in many respects, has made it much more difficult for the U.S. government to evade responsibility for its actions.

In my own long career of teaching and research, I have come to appreciate Eisenhower's boldness. In pointing out the links between the military and industry, he understood that any supposedly international issue—for example, arms sales or trading—has domestic, ethical ramifications. To be sure, corruption and malfeasance are habitual in politics. Ike's concern that the rise of the military-industrial complex would lead to a rise of "misplaced power" seems like an obvious observation now. One need only think of the wars in Iraq and Afghanistan as two current examples of that power. Ike would have much to say about the way that means distort ends in such conflicts. Certainly, he would not be surprised that the enhanced roles of private contractors in both military affairs have caused concern.

In terms of ethical aspects of war, peace, and national security, we are in a better place than we were in 1961, even though the reasons why are hard to see. To be optimistic requires us to remember that social change is difficult to map as it is occurring, and it is always lengthy and uneven. It would be decades before we would realize how parochial the mainstream scholarly literature of Eisenhower's era was. It would also be decades after his speech before we would acknowledge that minimizing ethical considerations in scholarship is every bit as damaging as neglecting them in the analysis of policy. Ike's time was one when American strategists like Herman Kahn asked if, in a world after nuclear war, "Will the living envy the dead?" This was as close as most theorists back then came to dealing with ethical concerns that might have an impact on national security. Today, such questions are explored in detail in both policy journals and more popular magazines.

To cite just one somewhat hackneyed example: we now consider whether a munitions factory should be kept open to protect U.S. jobs even though the weapons produced there might end up in the hands of leaders whose regimes are "enemies" of the U.S. That such a question is routinely debated in public conversation rather than confined to more esoteric university research seminars, and that international relations and its links to domestic politics are a subject of study, is a sign of progress. We may trace the broader exposure of these issues back to Ike's sobering analysis in 1961.

The often murky connections between the corporate world and the realm of high politics are the subject not only of obscure doctoral dissertations, but also of substantive investigative journalism. That is something to applaud. Again, we should acknowledge that Ike was among the first to articulate the challenge of non-state actors to defense and security affairs, as a result of his own personal experience from inside the military establishment.

**The U.S. and Other Countries**
When Ike spoke, the idea that the U.S. military-industrial complex could affect the Israeli-American relationship in deleterious ways was far from people's minds. That Israel would develop its own high-tech version of the military-industrial complex and that its political leaders would succumb to corrupt practices as a consequence was a future reality that was unforeseen in 1961.

Thanks to Eisenhower's warning, we can better understand that political leaders never fully appreciate the domestic political issues their counterparts in other countries face. Leaders of one country do not necessarily learn lessons about military goals and means from leaders of other countries, even if those lessons may seem obvious. Leaders of one country also never fully accept the assertions of "national security" other countries use as a justification for their actions or inaction. This is especially true in a complicated, bilateral relationship like that between Israel and the U.S., when the domestic politics of each country play as large a role in shaping the relationship as they do in dictating each country's own national security priorities.

If there are any "truths" in international relations, these observations constitute some of them. So we are still indebted to Ike for making plain that for all countries, not just for the U.S., there are dangers as well as opportunities in building economies and polities in which corporate actors and others assume responsibilities that had previously been more firmly established as under the domain of the democratic state.

**The Tasks Ahead**
In terms of prioritizing the ethical dilemmas that Jewish scholars must analyze, examining the extent to which political leaders abdicate responsibility for the consequences of their behavior must rank high. This is a task for all of us as citizens, not just as academics or just as Jews. Where do we begin?

One possibility is to look more critically at assertions that in recent decades, as Eisenhower warned, the U.S. has become infected with "the new militarism." A leading scholar of international relations, Andrew Bacevich, argues that America's domestic politics and its foreign policy betray a common infatuation with military solutions to complex problems ranging from employment, race relations, and poverty to energy security and global health. Reading a newspaper often confirms this diagnosis. We are exposed daily to the U.S. penchant for discussing "wars" on drugs, cancer, or environmental degradation.

So, a second possibility for working toward greater accountability for American policies would be to point out that this vocabulary may, in fact, have produced a kind of paralysis that leaves citizens thinking they are powerless to affect change, even as voters. Why? Because in "wars," citizens are taught to be deferential to either political or military leaders.

Admittedly, these two tasks are modest. Yet, they have potentially far-reaching consequences and are thus worthy as an initial step toward restoring both accuracy and civility to our discourse.

Eisenhower's candid observations long ago were meant to be a wake-up call. That call is still relevant today as we struggle to decide what kind of society we wish to become and to portray to those abroad. We live in a world of diverse societies whose leaders are increasingly less willing both to follow America's crusades and to subordinate their own domestic political agendas to international imperatives drafted in Washington.

## The Ethics of the Sale of Arms by Governments
Steven L. Spiegel

### The Rules of International Behavior

INTERNATIONAL POLITICS is the Hobbesian realm of the jungle, where everyone must protect themselves or fall prey to others. Reinhold Niebuhr and Hans Morgenthau, the great political writers of the middle of the 20th century, famously noted that, unlike in the domestic arena, on the world stage there are no procedures to enforce the law. Despite the existence of a variety of institutions in current world affairs that ostensibly have the power to enforce international regulations—from the ICC (International Criminal Court) to the EU (European Union) to the ICJ (the International Court of Justice)—countries adhere to such regulations only when they find it in their interests to do so. In other words, they play by the rules only when they want to play by the rules.

If you run a traffic light, you know, or should know, that your infraction is subject to a penalty should you be caught by a police officer or camera. In the international system, many countries will "run a red light" when they believe that no one is looking or that they will not suffer for their wrongdoing. In international politics, the question of whether a penalty should be imposed on aggressors and evildoers is determined by a variety of factors: the relative strength of the aggressor, that of the victim and the victim's allies, and whether the state(s) that has the capability to stop the aggressor believes it is in its interest to do so.

Today, many states are confronted with regional conflicts, such as those between India and Pakistan, Israel and Syria, Israel and Iran, North Korea and South Korea, and China and Taiwan. In some situations, a potential aggressor may be tempted to attack an apparently weak neighboring country, as Iraq's former President Saddam Hussein did to Kuwait in 1990. Therefore, states often try to maintain weapons designed not only to discourage potential opponents from attacking, but also to provide effective defense should deterrence fail. A state may enter into an alliance to bolster its position in the world and in the arms race.

In recent years, the situation has become even more complex because new threats have developed—asymmetric threats, such as those used on 9/11 and in suicide bombings not only by foreign terrorists, but also by citizens of the targeted country. Such attacks have happened in many countries, including Afghanistan, Pakistan, Spain, England, Israel, and Iraq. They are responsible for dozens, even hundreds of deaths, and require different types of weapons and tactics to thwart.

## Are Arms Sales Moral?

The violent nature of international politics brings us to the question of arms sales. The central question about the morality of these sales is whether they contribute to the defense of states from acts of aggression by other states or from terrorist acts inside their borders.

It is expensive to develop weapons, so states that have the technical capacity to do so attempt to reduce that cost by selling weapons to other countries. For example, Israel (with American assistance) is currently seeking to develop more sophisticated anti-ballistic missiles, especially of short-range capacity, that could be used to counter southern missile attacks by Hamas or Islamic Jihad from Gaza or northern attacks by Hezbollah from Lebanon. This is a financially draining undertaking, and Israel will undoubtedly try to sell some of the missiles when they are ready for installation. Similarly, instruments used for anti-terrorist purposes (e.g., drones, motion and metal detectors, facial recognition software, defensive systems like "iron dome" for shooting down rockets) are also expensive candidates for sale to other nations threatened by terrorism.

Are these exchanges moral? The development and sale of arms inherently spread the use of those arms, resulting in injuries and deaths. The arms trade is thus repulsive and, without specific justification, immoral. At the same time, however, countries that are victims of state-sponsored attacks or independent acts of terrorism, or are under credible threat, have a moral imperative to protect their own citizens. Furthermore, if a country like the U.S. or Israel can help a country that is a fellow victim of terrorism, is it not a higher moral imperative to do so than to keep its hands clean by flatly refusing to share weapons? Beyond morality, the dynamics of self-interest may argue in favor of the transfer of weapons. When a country participates in the sale of arms, it may build a reputation of being well-armed, discouraging aggressors from attacking it for fear of retaliation. Arms sales certainly help countries stay well-armed, so that they may defeat aggressors who do attack. One could thus plausibly argue that, according to morality or self-interest, it is better to provide arms than not to, in order to discourage the use of violence in global conflicts.

On the other hand, what if these weapons actually make the situation worse by encouraging a potential victim of aggression or terrorism to act in a more offensive manner? There can never be certainty about how arms will be used, except for weapons that can only be used defensively (e.g., anti-ballistic missiles), and that creates an inherent tension between the potential positive and negative consequences of trading weaponry. But states also consider the financial and political consequences of the sales themselves, so it is a complex calculation that produces decisions about whether or not to sell arms. The key point here is that a consideration of moral impact *must* be part of that decision-making process.

**The Reality of Arms Sales**

This moral, financial, and political calculus becomes hopelessly complex in practice. For example, when the U.S. sells arms to Israel, most Americans believe that activity is not only morally justified, but also morally right because Israel is a U.S. ally surrounded by a number of its adversaries. However, critics of Israel in America and abroad who believe that it is guilty of human rights violations toward the Palestinians will argue against U.S. arms sales to Israel based on that moral measure.

Both the U.S. and Israel have been questioned about their sales of arms to a variety of countries, such as China, India, and Latin America. Is China an appropriate customer for arms, for instance? On the one hand, these sales might keep Beijing from moving into an aggressive and isolationist policy toward Taiwan, and might induce cooperation with the U.S. over crafting policies to discourage North Korean nuclear development. On the other hand, because of its policies toward Taiwan and human rights violations involving both Tibet and its own citizenry, arms should perhaps not be sold to China. Israel has consistently sold weapons to China over the last several years, often to the consternation of Washington. By contrast, the U.S. has maintained a ban on selling weapons to Beijing since the Tiananmen Square massacre of 1989, demonstrating the difficult calculations states make in particular cases according to their differing interests and military situations.

In many cases, if a country is denied the arms that it seeks to buy from one country, it can go elsewhere to purchase weapons. For example, the American rationale for arms sales to Saudi Arabia has been to keep others from selling their arms to the Saudis, so that the U.S. can control the number and sophistication of Saudi weapons. The U.S. has maintained that the Saudis were willing to accept these limitations because of their strong need for closer relations with Washington. Thus, arms sales can be justified, as in the Saudi example, on the grounds that they promote diplomacy, international cooperation, and even the restraint of the recipient state.

Such an example also illustrates that it can be more moral to sell arms to controversial countries as a means of controlling their future behavior than not to sell arms at all. Some therefore maintain that the profit the seller makes by reducing the cost of its weaponry, thus increasing the volume of its sales, is less important than the diplomatic and security benefits gained from those sales. This has certainly been true for Israel, especially regarding its arms sales to such countries as India and China.

Of course, there are many cases when the sale of arms cannot be justified under any circumstances, as in the cases of sales to such countries as Sudan and Myanmar (Burma). Their egregious actions toward their own citizens and neighbors are so outrageous that no rationale could justify selling arms to them.

In sum, arms development, production, and sales are inherently immoral except when they are regarded as critical to self-defense and preservation. An important proviso is that countries must consider the ethical impact of arms sales. Hence, there should be times when they refuse to sell weapons because the states that seek them are deemed too dangerous. In this sense, the potential use of weapons after they are sold should always be considered and the costs and benefits of their use should be weighed. Countries should also consider inserting clauses in their sales contracts to control the use of weapons they sell.

For example, cluster bombs (which the U.S. has sold to Israel, among other countries) are particularly lethal weapons for two reasons. First, a cluster bomb delivers multiple bombs that scatter upon launch. When used in urban areas, the cluster bomb explodes in midair, spreading bomblets across a large area, usually killing civilians. Second, many of these bomblets remain undetonated on impact, sitting like landmines and causing casualties even once fighting has ceased. Therefore, cluster bombs should be sold only under extraordinary conditions to countries in critical need of them for self-defense. The selling country should always be careful to require in the terms of sale that the buyers will use such weapons only under the direst of circumstances and in the situations for which they were designed, particularly for use in tank warfare.

Israel has sometimes been accused, as it was in 2006 in Lebanon, of using this type of weapon inappropriately. But in such cases, the Israeli government has responded vehemently that it has abided by the agreements it made with the U.S. when it bought these weapons, to employ them only in battlefield situations.

The issue of money's role in arms sales is always complicated, subject to a variety of moral questions. Suffice it to say that, at least in theory, countries should not pursue arms development for profit, but only for defense. It should go without saying that the human rights policies of the purchasers and the justice of their motives should be major considerations for a country in deciding whether to sell to them. Of course, if arms sales are employed simply to enrich arms contractors—a problem prevalent in the United States—then they cannot be justified on any grounds.

The only acceptable justification for arms sales is that they often contribute critically to the defense of both the seller and the buyer, enabling the producing country to share the cost of developing weapons and, at the same time, helping deserving countries to defend themselves. The critical point here is that arms should not be sold simply to benefit arms sellers and/or producers. If these sales are meant only to make arms contractors richer or to make it easier for either the seller or the buyer to commit acts of aggression, then they are simply wrong.

**Nuclear Proliferation**

To the best of the public's knowledge, neither the U.S. nor Israel has ever sold nuclear weapons to other countries. This is especially the case with Israel, which has never officially admitted possessing nuclear weapons in the first place. It is also inconceivable that either country would sell these weapons out of self-interest, as that may encourage the purchasing country or other countries to develop nuclear weapons of their own. There also can never be a guarantee that a country buying these weapons will not transfer them to a third country, or that its regime will not change, as it did in Iran when the Shah fell, after years of arms trading and cooperation in nuclear development with America.

Of course, nuclear technology is different from conventional weaponry because nuclear energy has civilian, as well as military, uses. As we have seen in many cases, however, the two can be confused. A country like Iran can claim that it is developing nuclear capabilities for civilian energy production when, in reality, it has a weapons program in mind. In contrast, in the case of conventional weapons, there is often no ancillary technology that has a positive corollary.

The U.S. is one of the leading anti-proliferation countries in the world. It is committed to preventing any further states from acquiring nuclear weapons, in the belief that any additional nuclear states would increase global instability. The U.S. has, however, used the transfer of nuclear technology in a controlled manner to persuade North Korea and Libya to enter into agreements to end their nuclear programs. In the case of Libya, in an agreement reached in 2003, the U.S. and its allies agreed to allow the country a certain type of civilian nuclear plant—one that is difficult to convert to nuclear weapons production—in exchange for its promise to dismantle its entire nuclear program.

A similar deal was reached with North Korea under the Clinton administration in 1994. However, after being accused of reneging on the agreement by the George H. W. Bush administration, North Korea intensified its nuclear production and, in the ensuing years, developed six to ten nuclear weapons. The George W. Bush administration then reversed its policy in 2006, and by 2007, a new agreement was reached. By 2008, North Korea, despite some steps backward, was dismantling its fledgling nuclear program in exchange for a variety of forms of assistance, including shipments of oil and the release of frozen funds. But then this new agreement also collapsed, and North Korea has become a nuclear danger once again, conveying mixed signals to the international community.

I believe that the Bush administration did not properly handle signs that North Korea was violating its agreement to halt nuclear development, which made finding a resolution with the country's government in Pyongyang more difficult. I still think that the sale of civilian nuclear reactors that are difficult to convert to weapons production is an effective means of preventing nuclear proliferation, though this avenue must be pursued with the greatest of care and caution.

A major question concerning this issue has been whether to assist countries that claim to want help in developing the capability to produce nuclear power for civilian use. The global community has been wrestling with this question since the 1950s. Such assistance was specifically allowed in the international Nuclear Non-Proliferation Treaty of 1968. Thus, aiding countries seeking to develop nuclear programs to expand their energy supplies has been considered acceptable, so long as proper international inspection protocols are followed and the assistance does not result in the expansion of nuclear development to create a weapons program.

On the other hand, the civilian option is inherently controversial in many cases, as illustrated by several contemporary examples. For instance, the current government in Iran has, with little credibility, maintained that it is merely developing a civilian nuclear energy program, not nuclear weapons. Many Arab regimes have suddenly developed an interest in building their own civilian nuclear energy programs, in response to the concern over Iran's potential nuclear weapons capabilities. In another controversial case, for all its opposition to a nuclear Indian presence, the Bush administration made a major agreement with India to help it develop civilian nuclear energy, which it claimed would enhance the two countries' relations and prevent the expansion of Indian nuclear weapons capabilities.

Some scholars and analysts argue that the proliferation of nuclear weapons can actually be positive in that it discourages countries from engaging in full-scale conflict because of the enormous damage that nuclear weapons can inflict. For example, in the Indian-Pakistani relationship, despite the enormous conflict between the two countries since Pakistan gained its independence in 1947, they avoid war (despite terrorist attacks and outbreaks of violence) largely because of the nuclear threat. However, the argument that nuclear proliferation acts as a deterrent to conflict is somewhat far-fetched, because it suggests the more dangerous the situation seems in terms of a nuclear threat, the safer it is in reality. This claim ignores the probability that the more states develop nuclear weapons, the more likely it will be that a nuclear accident will occur or that some kind of nuclear war will break out.

In sum, sharing nuclear weapons with another country can never be justified on either moral or political grounds. Yet, the sale of conventional weapons and cooperation to develop civilian nuclear energy, even when undertaken to prevent the development of the nuclear military option, are activities with complicated moral repercussions. Thus, governments must judge only on a case-by-case basis whether or not to sell arms or offer assistance in nuclear development to other countries.

In general, safeguards often make sharing civilian nuclear know-how harmless, but it can carry implications that reach beyond national and global security. American involvement in the exchange of civilian nuclear technology can be justified with the argument that the United States will impose tougher safeguards than other countries will, demanding more frequent and more thorough inspections. That said, it would still be both more moral and more advisable to devote American efforts to developing renewable sources of energy (wind, solar, etc.), rather than relying on nuclear power to meet the growing demand for alternatives to fossil fuels. This would reduce the potential danger of nuclear weapons by reducing demand for the production of nuclear energy and prevent environmental hazards resulting from nuclear waste or accidents.

Finally, should the U.S. sell conventional weapons to prevent other countries from going nuclear? That option is also filled with dangers, because once a country begins to negotiate in these terms, it is often difficult to figure out where to draw the line. What if a potential nuclear state keeps asking for increasingly sophisticated conventional weapons in exchange for its continued abstinence from nuclear development? Moreover, advanced conventional weapons do not provide the prestige and deterrence capabilities afforded by nuclear weapons. Thus, the chances of completely replacing the nuclear arms trade with the conventional arms trade are low.

Although there will necessarily be exceptions, it is better not to sell one type of weapon in order to offset the production of another type of weapon. Nations should only sell for the reasons set forth in this essay, those critical to the defense of both the seller and the buyer. In any case, arms sales are a necessary component of the current anarchic international system. The best we can do is to take a prudent approach to arms sales that takes both morality and self-interest into account in a balanced and cautious manner, keeping in mind the centrality of defense—not profit—as the motivation for these types of transactions.

## The Complex Relationship between the Military and the Economy: An Interview with Richard Immerman

Julia Oestreich

*This is the transcript of an interview that Julia Oestreich conducted with Richard Immerman in Philadelphia on September 30, 2009.*

**Julia Oestreich: As former Assistant Deputy Director of National Intelligence for Analytic Integrity and Standards and Analytic Ombudsman for the office of the Director of National Intelligence, you have had some direct experience with the way that the military is funded and also with the way that politics takes hold when it comes to the interplay between money and the military, correct?**

**Richard Immerman:** Yes, and in fact, most of what I would say here comes from my work. The relationship between the military and civil society, which is to some extent what you're dealing with in the case study, is telescoped in certain ways. It demonstrates that the intelligence community is unusual in a number of different ways.

First of all, the office of the Director of National Intelligence supervises 16 different elements of the intelligence community including the Defense Intelligence Agency, which theoretically oversees intelligence for the entire military. But the Navy has its own independent intelligence agency, whereas the CIA and the FBI are independent of the military.

But it's more complicated than that because the Pentagon controls about 80% to 90% of the intelligence budget. So even though, for example, the National Security Agency is under the leadership of the Director of National Intelligence, it's also under the aegis of the Secretary of Defense, because the money for satellites and other necessary intelligence devices comes from the Pentagon. So it's a very mixed and imperfect structure, and I would always be aware of it because I would go to national intelligence board meetings and half the people would come in in uniform.

That is not how the intelligence community is supposed to be. It is supposed to be a civil, non-military organization. But this is the way it is, and there are consequences to that—not necessarily in terms of the military-industrial complex as conventionally understood, but because of the influence that the Pentagon in particular has over the budget. And therefore, because money is power, the Pentagon has a huge effect

Case 4: Responses

not only on American intelligence activities, but also ultimately on the American economy as a whole.

**JO: So do you think that the economy, beyond being tied in with the military, is to a certain degree dependent upon the military?**

**RI:** You know, at this point it is dependent, and I would say that we should think seriously about incorporating private contractors into this discussion. Contractors make the government work now. If you hang around Washington and military intelligence, the contracting companies are absolutely mammoth. To give you an example, in my office I had 12 personnel to supervise 30 contractors. That gives you a sense of the numbers.

In the military-industrial complex, it used to be like a pipeline: You would be in the military, and then you'd go to work for a corporation that was a military supplier. Now, you actually go to work for a contractor, and that contractor works for the military—including, for example, the guys who were in Iran, Blackwater and Halliburton. Some of those companies have former industrial names. In other words, they're no longer producing supplies like aircraft; they became contractors, so they're providing services for the military.

McDonnell Douglas does contracting work; they're all over the place, and that relationship is incredible. So, certainly, I think one could argue that there's a certain degree of impact on the relationship between the military and the economy as a result of these contracts. "Dependent" is a hard word to parse, but with these military contractors money flows back and forth, and you end up with companies like Halliburton.

There are two things to keep in mind about how we perceive the relationship between the military and the economy: one is to be careful about the type of reductionist thinking that says, "Okay, this guy was in the army. He then went onto this board and therefore they're all in bed together." A lot of the guys who work for contractors believe strongly in the national interest, but they do have an expertise gained from experience, and they go back and forth between the military and corporate worlds. Their value is in that experience, not necessarily in their influence.

The other thing is, Aaron Friedberg has written a book, *In the Shadow of the Garrison State*, on the military-industrial complex. He argues that what has been remarkable about American civil society, particularly during the Cold War, is that the military-industrial complex has been so small despite the perception of military threats and given the defense spending to meet those threats. That's because Americans do believe in separation of powers—I mean liberty—and a limited government that curtails its power, compared to, let's say, the Soviet Union, whose military-industrial complex was humongous to the point that there was no distinction between powers because of the state system and how that worked.

But there certainly is this nexus, this relationship, between the military and industry in America, based on individuals, based on how the contracts work. You know, there are only a certain number of companies that are large enough to be able to service the needs of the military. So it's not as if I could build the Abrams tank, send it out for bidding, and many different companies would bid on the work. There are only a few companies that have the capacity to produce or pay for the right equipment. So it's hard to imagine their not having some sort of influence on government procurement.

It's obviously in the interest of these companies to get a former general to work for them because he's going to know someone else. And they do get them. The companies have cooling-off periods, where you can't lobby a government agency, or perhaps a military branch, where you formerly worked for a specified amount of time. But these safeguards are not foolproof. There is no "cooling-off period" for sharing expertise.

**JO: Do you think that the relationships you're talking about may actually make us more predisposed to involvement in military conflict?**

**RI:** No. I don't see it, at least not decisively. To begin with, conflicts themselves are not necessarily good for business. The money comes from research and development. That's where it is, and that's a constant flow. Many countries are different, so it's not as if when we blow up or lose however many weapons or supplies, we're going to be able to build that many more of them and resupply them. For one thing, it takes a long time to do that—the acquisition happens way ahead of time. Where I think there's a more dramatic impact is not on the conflict itself, but in the research, in the threat perception, and therefore in the development and acquisition of weaponry.

Take Star Wars, for example. Star Wars was a defensive notion; that was at least the idea behind it. Even so, it was clearly not perceived by the Soviet Union at that time as defensive. It's often difficult to distinguish between what's offensive and what's defensive. That ambiguity will often precipitate a response, a reaction. That's called "the security dilemma"—you build your thing up, and I'm going to build something bigger. And because of that, if I'm a defense contractor, I'm in hog heaven. I want you to just keep ordering weapons.

War doesn't really affect that dynamic in many ways, and you could argue that unless you have a peace dividend (in which the government redirects appropriations from military to non-military spending), which has never panned out, war doesn't necessarily increase the profits of these sorts of companies. If you were to ask me whether this type of competitive relationship fueled a sense of vulnerability, of threat, and therefore perpetuated the need to respond and build up weaponry, I'd say yes, I can see that. But that doesn't mean actually going over that precipice to war, because I don't think any one of these companies really wants a war or really needs a war to succeed financially.

**JO: My next question is a multi-part question. I'll start by saying that a lot of people argue that military expenditures take up too large a piece of the pie.**

**RI:** There are *lots* of people who argue that.

**JO: So my first question would be: Do you feel that the large amount of resources allocated for the military is necessary?**

**RI:** The answer is no, and particularly in the current climate. American military capability is so vastly superior to any other competitor that unless you believe, and some do, that the United States has to maintain that superiority forever, we do not need to maintain the current level of spending for the military. If the goal is deterrence, we're way beyond what is necessary for deterrence.

But I won't blame our excessive military spending exclusively on the military-industrial complex. There is no question that it's good for business, and no one's going to say, "Stop." But the perception of real threats to our security is certainly, I think, engrained in the consciousness of many of our decision makers, not just in the military, but in the civilian sphere, too. So, for example, Dick Cheney didn't develop his world view because he worked for Halliburton. What he ended up doing for Halliburton stemmed from what he already believed. Therefore, it became almost natural that he would work for Halliburton. Halliburton would want him to work for them; there was congruence there.

I think people tend to see the military-industrial complex in some sort of conspiratorial way, that it is leading people in ways they otherwise would not go. I think it's just a part of political culture, particularly the political culture around national security matters. The military people who go back and forth between military and civilian life have contacts, so they can talk to people on both sides. I think that's important, even if it ends up feeding into the so-called military-industrial complex.

**JO: So what do you think we lose or neglect by spending as much as we do on the military?**

**RI:** I don't know if, let's say, changing military spending would affect the health care debate except at the margins. The issues in that debate tend to be ideological as much as anything else. Wealthy people resent paying for the health care of those with less, and owners of small businesses know that money saved from cancelling a certain weapons system is not going to help pay the health care for their workers.

But military spending affects infrastructural types of things, education being one, rapid transit being another. Now, in many places, people would argue that we already missed the boat. In other words, the cost of putting in a certain type of rail system is so prohibitively expensive that we're not going to do it. Well, leaving aside whether or not we might have been able to spend on infrastructure if we didn't spend so much on the military, the argument is always that you cannot put a price tag on national security, so that money will always be spent.

But that certainly decreases the likelihood that money is going to flow to a city for urban needs, for example. This was all the more so in the post-Reagan years, as the budget went more into deficit and people got more adamant that the budget had to be balanced as Keynesian economics retreated. Ultimately, it becomes almost a zero-sum game, so military spending has to have an effect. And it's easier, frankly, particularly after 9/11, to get people to support spending tax dollars for security than it is to get them to pay for schools, rapid transit, or environmental measures.

**JO: Do you think anything is gained by constantly devoting so many resources to the military or by keeping it at the top of the priority list?**

**RI:** Well, I think that there are those who argue, particularly in today's world, that you need to maintain a credible military, a "second strike" capability, so if you bomb me, I can get you back. As a student of international relations and security, I could say yes, we need that. Fine, but that's totally different from what the reality is now. Given the amount of money spent on certain strategic defense initiatives, particularly since you often can't even define what is a threat, I would say that that money could be used more effectively in other ways. If you accept my premise that, to some extent, it is a zero-sum game, then it could be used for other priorities.

**JO: Considering some of the things you've already mentioned about the way that the military has to function now, focusing more on things like deterrence, the fact that now we're focusing on individual terrorists, terrorist acts, and terrorist organizations as much as we focus on potentially dangerous regimes, how does the need to spend on the military change? And how is the way money is allocated to different military resources affected?**

**RI:** Well, there are a couple of things. There was once the notion or the hope that we could rely on technology, both as a source of intelligence (which is critical to the military enterprise), as well as for deterrence. As non-state actors have become a more salient threat, that changes how much is spent on technology, for which, no matter how much you spend on it, you end up spending more. Once you spend more, it's a fixed cost.

There are increased costs in having an all-volunteer army, in terms of the maintenance and deployment of conventional forces and the premium on human assets for gathering intelligence, and these costs are ever-expanding. Quite frankly, the cost of recruitment and advertising has gone up. So you have increasingly expensive technology getting all the more sophisticated (such as cyber warfare), and yet the human cost of recruitment and training seems to be getting more expensive than the technology.

**JO: Is the competition for more advanced weapons and military technology a positive development?**

**RI:** Well, there's a long history of the application of military technology to civilian use. That was the argument behind the moon race—those technologies have civilian uses too. And I think, to some extent, that's true. However, there are other technologies where I think that the spill-off is probably less, where they aren't applicable to civilian use.

Given that you try to look ahead, what is the technology going to be 25 years from now? What are we going to develop to counter that? This is what I was involved with as Assistant Deputy Director of National Intelligence for Analytic Integrity and Standards: Here's a new technology that has been developed. What is its potential? And then, suddenly there's a lot of money that's going to be spent to develop some counter to a technology that hasn't even been developed yet. Well, of course, that's an unending process.

And it takes an awful lot of political will, something I've hardly ever seen in Congress, at least, for someone to say, "You know, this is so far down the road, we don't know what the technology will be like. We're not going to do it." Instead, when in doubt, we fund it. And that takes a lot of money. The more advanced the technology has gotten, the greater the impetus to keep ahead of that curve, and that costs that much more money. But it's understandable—better safe than sorry.

**JO: So considering that that technological race is constantly going on, how does nuclear non-proliferation play in?**

**RI:** It's really hard. Nuclear non-proliferation is a value. But I think, to some extent, it's hard to argue with those who say that, in a world of growing anarchy, our own nuclear defense leads to the possibility not only of rogue states obtaining nuclear weapons, but of terrorists getting them. So the need is for more countermeasures, counter-terrorist types of measures, to prevent that from happening. Non-proliferation is such a difficult thing to try to orchestrate at this point.

**JO: Do you think it's worth pursuing?**

**RI:** I don't know what the alternative is, unless you accept the view of some political scientists that the safest thing would be if absolutely everyone has a nuclear weapon, and then there will be all this self-deterrence. Not many of us are willing to go that far. There are ways to proceed: set target dates for incremental "disarmament," and then institute verification regimes. Yet, the country that disarms can still retain more than sufficient capabilities to deter or retaliate against outside aggression. But we don't live in an environment conducive to "big thinking."

**JO: In light of everything we've discussed about the relationship between the military and the economy, is peace economically viable? And what is our responsibility to balance competing**

**interests of staying militarily and technologically competitive, keeping Americans safe, but trying to encourage peace?**

**RI:** I'd make the argument that, of course, peace is viable. War or conflict is usually not economically productive, at least in the long run. There can be short-term gains for some. But ultimately, war does not lead to the kind of structural development on which economic prosperity can be sustained.

What is more, almost regardless of the international environment at any given time, nations will have security concerns—and therefore they will prepare for the worst. At a minimum they will seek to deter potential adversaries. Many thus argue that the most we can ever expect is stability—hence, they define peace as the absence of war. Especially given the technological advances that have become so common today, this dynamic will keep defense industries employed. And technological advances in times of peace are more likely to be converted for civilian use—and benefit. If you define peace this way, then I think it is certainly economically sustainable.

This also brings us back to the notion of the military-industrial complex. The so-called "garrison state," which functions primarily to maintain military power, almost by definition stifles entrepreneurship and venture capitalism, if only because it requires so much of the budget to be spent on the military. It is certainly not a boon to economic growth. Indeed, the types of wage and price controls imposed during war prove to be a constraint, regardless of the maximal employment created by the constant need for war production. Hence, again, this argues against those who see peace as something that will retard, as opposed to stimulate, the economy.

The bottom line is that most Americans believe strongly in a set of core values—values that are, in most cases, antithetical to the "garrison state."

# Conclusion: The Ethics of War and National Security

WAR IS, of course, a wrenchingly difficult subject that demands serious thought and consideration. Among the issues that are central to any theory on the morality of war are the balancing of national security with freedom, justifications for war, rules of conduct during war, and the relationship between war and the formation of national policies.

How should Judaism influence the way that we formulate our own views of war? As we indicated in the Introduction, Jews have not had much historical experience in waging war and in responding to the questions that it raises. As such, we cannot just cite authoritative texts and deduce what we should do from them. Rather, we need to plumb the Jewish tradition for its underlying values. These include the following:

- the sanctity of every human being as created in the image of God
- the obligation to protect our own lives and health
- the consequent duty to defend ourselves against attack
- the responsibility to come to the aid of anyone whose life or health is threatened
- the strong ties that each of us has with our community, and the duty to take an active role in the decisions and policies of that community
- the sense that war is not to be undertaken lightly: in traditional sources, wars were permitted only when the Sanhedrin (the supreme Rabbinic court) and God (through divinations of the High Priest) agreed to them; while in modern times, it is not clear what, if any, process authorizes Jews to go to war
- the obligation to fix the world to the extent that we can to avoid the conditions that lead to war
- the duty to seek peace and pursue it

Intelligent, morally sensitive, and Jewishly committed people may well differ on the issues that this volume raises. This, of course, is true of any modern moral issue. But it is especially true however for matters of war and peace—where life and death hang in the balance—about which we have so little guidance from our tradition, and which become even more ethically complex and dangerous with each technological advance.

At the turn of the 20th century, the relative lack of widespread military conflict in Europe led many people to hope that they could live in a world without war. This dream, of course, collapsed with the advent of World War I, and the 20th century ultimately witnessed some of the most horrific wars that humanity has ever experienced, in both the sheer numbers of people who died and the depth of depravity displayed in the conduct of the warring soldiers and governments. Unfortunately, the 21st century has not started out with much promise for changing this record.

Consequently, however difficult it may be to address the issues in this volume, it is absolutely critical that we do so—the future of humanity is at stake. We hope that this book has helped you to start this task.

# Suggestions for Further Reading

## National Security

Dershowitz, Alan M. *Is There a Right to Remain Silent: Coercive Interrogation and the Fifth Amendment After 9/11*. Oxford: Oxford University Press, 2008. Inalienable Rights Series, Series Editor Geoffrey R. Stone.

Dorff, Elliot N. *Love Your Neighbor and Yourself: A Jewish Approach to Modern Personal Ethics*. Philadelphia: The Jewish Publication Society, 2003, especially chapter 2, "Privacy."

Ignatieff, Michael. *The Lesser Evil: Political Ethics in an Age of Terror*. Toronto: Penguin Canada, 2004.

Lamm, Norman. "The Right of Privacy." In *Judaism and Human Rights*. Milton R. Konvitz, ed. New York: W.W. Norton & Company, Inc., 1972. The B'nai B'rith Jewish Heritage Classics, Series Editors David Patterson and Lily Edelman, 233.

Lerner, Michael, ed. *Best Jewish Writing 2002*. San Francisco: Jossey-Bass, 2002, see the section of essays entitled "Jewish Response to September 11th."

Netanyahu, Benjamin. *Fighting Terrorism: How Democracies Can Defeat Domestic and International Terrorists*. New York: Noonday Press, 1995.

Netanyahu, Benjamin ed. *Terrorism: How the West Can Win*. New York: Farrar, Straus and Giroux, 1986.

Pedahzur, Ami and Arie Perleger. *Jewish Terrorism in Israel*. New York: Columbia University Press, 2009.

Tal, Israel. *National Security: The Israeli Experience*. Westport, CT: Praeger Publishers, 2000.

## Justifications for War

Artson, Bradley Shavit. *Love Peace and Pursue Peace: A Jewish Response to War and Nuclear Annihilation.* New York: United Synagogue of America, 1988.

Dorff, Elliot. "'A Time for War and a Time for Peace': The Ethics of War and International Intervention." *To Do the Right and the Good: A Jewish Approach to Modern Social Ethics.* Philadelphia: The Jewish Publication Society, 2002.

Goldberg, Edwin C. *Swords and Plowshares: Jewish Views of War and Peace*. New York: URJ Press, 2006.

Greenberg, Irving. "The Ethics of Jewish Power." In *Beyond Occupation*. Marc H. Ellis and Rosemary Radford Reuther, eds. Boston: Beacon Press, 1990, 22–74.

Homolka, Walter, and Albert Friedlander. *The Gate to Perfection: The Idea of Peace in Jewish Thought.* New York: Berghahn Books, 1994.

Katz, Stephen, ed. "War." In *Frontiers of Jewish Thought.* Washington, DC: B'nai Brith Books, 1992.

Shapiro, David. "The Jewish Attitude Toward War and Peace." In *Studies in Jewish Thought, Volume 1*. New York: Yeshiva University Press, 1975.

Walzer, Michael. *Just and Unjust Wars: A Moral Argument with Historical Illustrations*. New York: Basic Books, 1977.

Walzer, Michael, ed. *Law, Politics, and Morality in Judaism*. Princeton, NJ: Princeton University Press, 2006, especially Part III, "War and Peace."

## The Conduct of War

Bleich, J. David. "Torture and the Ticking Bomb." *Tradition* 39, No. 4 [2006], 89–121.

Broyde, Michael J. "Jewish Law and Torture." *New York Jewish Week* [July 7, 2006].

Crane, Jonathan K. "With a Mighty Hand: Judaic Ethics of Exercising Power in Extraordinary Warfare." *Enemy Combatants, Terrorism, and Armed Conflict Law: A Guide to the Issues*. David K. Linnan, ed. Westport, CT: Praeger Security International, 2008, 184–206.

———. *Modern Jewish Ethical Discourse.* Forthcoming.

Feld, Edward. "Developing a Jewish Theology Regarding Torture." *Theology Today* 63 (2006), 324–329. Republished in Hunsinger (2008), cited below, 145–151.

Hunsinger, George. *Torture Is a Moral Issue: Christians, Jews, Muslims, and People of Conscience Speak Out*. Grand Rapids, MI: Eerdmans, 2008.

Ish-Shalom, Benjamin. "Purity of Arms' and Purity of Ethical Judgment." In *Meorot* 6, No. 1 (2006), 1–9.

Klapper, Aryeh. "Warfare, Ethics and Jewish Law." In *Meorot* 6, No. 1 (2006), 3–9.

Landes, Daniel, ed. *Confronting Omnicide: Jewish Reflections on Weapons of Mass Destruction.* Northvale, NJ: Jason Aronson, 1991.

Luban, David. "Human Dignity, Humiliation, and Torture." In *Kennedy Institute of Ethics Journal* 19, No. 3 (2009), 211–230.

Matthews, Richard. *The Absolute Violation: Why Torture Must Be Prohibited.* Montreal: McGill-Queen's University Press, 2008.

Novak, David. "Nuclear War and the Prohibition of Wanton Destruction." *Jewish Social Ethics.* New York: Oxford University Press, 1992.

Passamaneck, Stephen M. *Police Ethics and the Jewish Tradition.* Springfield, IL: Charles C. Thomas, 2003.

Schiffman, Lawrence and Joel B. Wolowelsky, eds. *War and Peace in the Jewish Tradition.* New York: Yeshiva University Press, 2007. The Orthodox Forum Series, Series Editor, Robert S. Hirt.

Shapira, Avaraham and Henry Near, eds. *The Seventh Day: Soldiers Talk about the Six-Day War.* New York: Charles Scribner's Sons, 1970 [an English translation of *Si'ah Lohamim, A Discussion of the Fighters,* published in Hebrew in 1967].

Yisraeli, Shaul. "Extradition." *Jewish Law: Examining Halacha, Jewish Issues and Secular Law.* Available at www.jlaw.com/Articles/extradition.html. Also printed in *Crossroads: Halacha and the Modern World, Vol. 3* (Alon Shvut-Gush Etzion, Israel: Zomet Institute), 191–202.

Zakheim, Dov S. "Confronting Evil: Terrorists, Torture, the Military and Halakhah." *Meorot* 6, No. 1 (2006), 3–21.

## National Policies Concerning War

Ellis, Marc. *Israel and Palestine Out of the Ashes: The Search for Jewish Identity in the Twenty-First Century.* Sterling, VA: Pluto Press, 2002.

Hartman, David. *Conflicting Visions: Spiritual Possibilities of Modern Israel.* New York: Schocken, 1990, esp. 231–242.

Kimelman, Reuven. "The Ethics of National Power: Government and War from the Sources of Judaism." *Perspectives* [February 1987].

Plaskow, Judith. "Israel: Toward a New Concept of Community." *Standing Again at Sinai.* San Francisco and New York: HarperCollins, 1991, 107–120.

Ramon, Einat. "The Ethics of Ruling a State with a Large Non-Jewish Minority." *Contemporary Jewish Ethics and Morality: A Reader.* Elliot N. Dorff and Louis E. Newman, eds. New York: Oxford University Press, 1995, 441–453.

Vorspan, Albert and David Saperstein. *Tough Choices: Jewish Perspectives on Social Justice.* New York: UAHC Press, 1992, especially chapter 7, "Peace and International Affairs."

# Editors and Contributors

## Editors

***Elliot N. Dorff,*** Rabbi (Jewish Theological Seminary), PhD (Columbia University), is rector and Sol and Anne Dorff Distinguished Professor of Philosophy at the American Jewish University (formerly the University of Judaism) in Los Angeles. Among the twelve books he has written are four award-winning books on Jewish ethics and law published by The Jewish Publication Society: *Matters of Life and Death* (1998) on Jewish medical ethics; *To Do the Right and the Good* (2002) on Jewish social ethics; *Love Your Neighbor and Yourself* (2003) on Jewish personal ethics; and *For the Love of God and People: A Philosophy of Jewish Law* (2007). He has also edited 10 books, including *Contemporary Jewish Ethics and Morality* (Oxford, 1995) and *Contemporary Jewish Theology* (Oxford, 1999), co-edited by Louis Newman, who also co-edited with Dorff the first three volumes of the *Jewish Choices, Jewish Voices* series. Since 1984, Rabbi Dorff has served on the Rabbinical Assembly's Committee on Jewish Law and Standards, and has served as its Chair since 2007. He has also served on several federal advisory commissions dealing with the ethics of health care, sexual responsibility, and research on human subjects. He is a member of the State of California's Ethics Committee on embryonic stem cell research. He is married to Marlynn, and they have four children and seven grandchildren.

***Danya Ruttenberg***, Rabbi (Ziegler School of Rabbinic Studies, American Jewish University), is the author of *Surprised By God: How I Learned to Stop Worrying and Love Religion* (Beacon Press, 2008), and editor of *The Passionate Torah: Sex and Judaism* (NYU Press, 2009) and *Yentl's Revenge: The Next Wave of Jewish Feminism* (Seal Press, 2001). She is also a contributing editor to *Lilith* and to the academic journal *Women and Judaism*, serves on the editorial board of *Sh'ma: A Journal of Jewish Responsibility* and Jewschool.com, and has been published in many books and periodicals over the years. Rabbi Ruttenberg, who lives in the Boston area with her husband and son, serves as the Senior Jewish Educator at Tufts University Hillel and teaches and lectures nationwide.

## Contributors

***Ari Brochin*** is a third-year student at the Benjamin N. Cardozo School of Law. He has worked on anti-discrimination litigation before the European Court of Human Rights and, before law school, was the founding executive director of the Union of Progressive Zionists (now JStreet U). He also spent two years at the Pardes Institute of Jewish Studies in Talpiot, Jerusalem.

**Sharon Brous,** rabbi (The Jewish Theological Seminary), is the founder of IKAR, a Jewish community in Los Angeles that integrates spiritual and religious practice with the pursuit of social justice. Listed among *The Forward's* 50 most influential American Jews and *Newsweek*'s leading rabbis in the country, she lectures and writes frequently about new trends in American religious life, next-generation engagement, and social justice. Sharon was a guest on National Public Radio's "Speaking of Faith" and is a panelist on *Newsweek* and *The Washington Post*'s online forum "On Faith."

**Noam Chomsky,** PhD (University of Pennsylvania), joined the staff of the Massachusetts Institute of Technology in 1955 and in 1961 was appointed full professor. In 1976, he was appointed Institute Professor in the Department of Linguistics and Philosophy. Chomsky has lectured at many universities in the U.S. and abroad, and is the recipient of numerous honorary degrees and awards. He has written and lectured widely on linguistics, philosophy, intellectual history, contemporary issues, international affairs, and U.S. foreign policy. His most recent books include *Rogue States: The Rule of Force in World Affairs* (South End, 2000); *Pirates and Emperors, Old and New: International Terrorism in the Real World* (Pluto Press, 2002); *Middle East Illusions* (Rowman and Littlefield, 2003); *Imperial Ambitions: Conversations on the Post-9/11 World* (Metropolitan Books, 2005); *What We Say Goes: Conversations on U.S. Power in a Changing World* (Metropolitan Books, 2007); and *The Essential Chomsky* (New Press, 2008).

**Donna Robinson Divine**, PhD (Columbia University), is the Morningstar Family Professor of Jewish Studies and Professor of Government at Smith College. She teaches Comparative Politics, Middle East Politics, and Political Theory, and holds a BA from Brandeis University. Fluent in Hebrew, Arabic, and Turkish, she has held visiting appointments at Yale, Harvard, and the Hebrew University and has won fellowships from the National Endowment of the Humanities and the Mellon Foundation, as well as several Fulbright grants. Having written many scholarly articles on Middle Eastern history and politics, she is also the author of several books, including *Politics and Society in Ottoman Palestine: The Arab Struggle for Survival and Power* (Lynne Rienner, 1994), *Postcolonial Theory and the Arab-Israeli Conflict* (Routledge, 2008), and *Exiled in the Homeland: Zionism and the Return to Mandate Palestine* (University of Texas Press, 2009).

**Steven Edelman-Blank**, rabbi (Ziegler School of Rabbinic Studies of the American Jewish University), is the rabbi of Tifereth Israel Congregation in Des

Moines, Iowa. A graduate of Harvard College, he also edited the Contemporary Sources of the first three volumes of the *Jewish Choices/Jewish Voices* series.

**Larry Greenfield**, JD (Georgetown University Law Center), served in the U.S. Naval Intelligence Reserves and lectures widely on American foreign policy and national security issues. He is Fellow in American Studies at the Claremont Institute for the Study of Statesmanship and Political Philosophy and Executive Director of the Reagan Legacy Foundation. Long active in Jewish life, he was also a Fellow of the Wexner Heritage Foundation.

**Richard Immerman**, PhD (Boston College), is Professor and Edward J. Buthusiem Family Distinguished Faculty Fellow in History at Temple University and the Marvin Wachman Director of its Center for the Study of Force and Diplomacy. He served as chair of the Department of History from 1998–2005. A former president of the Society for Historians of American Foreign Relations and winner of its Stuart Bernath Book and Lecture prizes, he has received the Board of Regents Excellence in Research Award from the University of Hawaii and the Paul W. Eberman Faculty Research Award from Temple. The author of many articles and co-editor of the *Oxford Handbook on the Cold War* (Oxford University Press, 2010), among his books are *Waging Peace: How Eisenhower Shaped an Enduring Cold War Strategy* (Oxford, 1998), and *Empire for Liberty: A History of American Imperialism from Benjamin Franklin to Paul Wolfowitz* (Princeton University Press, 2010). From September 2007 to December 2008, Immerman served as Assistant Deputy Director of National Intelligence for Analytic Integrity and Standards and Analytic Ombudsman for the Office of the Director of National Intelligence.

**Joseph Kashnow** grew up wanting to serve in the U.S. military. He finally realized his dream and enlisted in the Army in the summer of 2001 as a cavalry scout. Four months after graduating from Ft. Knox, and just a week after getting married, he was given orders to deploy to Iraq. After six months of battling the remnants of the Iraqi Army and the insurgency, Kashnow was wounded by a roadside bomb on September 17, 2003. He spent five days in an American military hospital in Germany before returning to the U.S., where he spent the next several years at Walter Reed Army Medical Center. He underwent two years of reconstructive surgery and, in 2005, his leg was amputated below the knee. While at Walter Reed, Kashnow and his wife Sarai established the Jewish Soldier Foundation (JSF) to support Jews in the U.S. military and help recruit Jews into the armed forces. He was able to work at the Pentagon for 18 months while completing his medical recovery. After a long battle to remain on active duty status, Kashnow retired from the Army in 2008, and now works for the federal government helping other wounded service members at Walter Reed find employment when they leave the military system.

**Linda B. Miller**, PhD (Columbia University), is professor emerita of Political Science at Wellesley College and adjunct professor of International Studies (Research) at the Watson Institute, Brown University. She edited the *International Studies Review* from 1998–2002 and is a co-editor of *Argentia*, published by the British International Studies Association. Widely published in American, British, and Israeli journals of international relations, her books include *Dynamics of World Politics: Studies in the Resolution of Conflict* (Prentice Hall, 1968); *Ideas and Ideals* (with Michael J. Smith, Westview Press, 1993); and *New Directions in U.S. Foreign Policy* (with Inderjeet Parmar and Mark Ledwidge, Routledge, 2009). She has held research appointments at Princeton, Harvard, Columbia, and Brown Universities, and fellowships from the Council on Foreign Relations, the Rockefeller Foundation, NATO, the Pew Trusts, and the Sloan Foundation.

**Seth Milstein** is a Lieutenant Colonel in the U.S. Marine Corps Reserve. A combat veteran from Operation Iraqi Freedom, he served as a Liaison Officer from the First Marine Expeditionary Force to the 1st Armoured Division (U.K.) during the invasion of Iraq. In his previous service on active duty, he deployed twice with the 15th Marine Expeditionary Unit to Southeast Asia and the Persian Gulf, where he was involved in responding to the U.S. Embassy bombings in Kenya and Tanzania, humanitarian operations in East Timor, and the war between Eritrea and Ethiopia. He is an investment banker in civilian life.

**Nadav Morag**, PhD (Tel Aviv University), is an associate professor of Political Science at the American Jewish University and senior research associate for the university's Center for Israel Studies. Dr. Morag also serves as a member of the Los Angeles and Orange County Sheriff's Departments' Homeland Security Advisory Council and is a member of the L.A. County Terrorism Early Warning Group. In 2001, Morag became Senior Director for Domestic Policy, and then Senior Director for Foreign Policy at Israel's National Security Council, where he was responsible for producing policy recommendations on matters of national security for then Prime Minister Ariel Sharon and his cabinet. He has authored articles and book chapters on terrorism, strategy, and the Middle East including "The National Military Strategic Plan for the War on Terrorism: An Assessment" in *Homeland Security Affairs* and "Unambiguous Ambiguity: The Opacity of the Oslo Peace Process" in *Israel: The First Hundred Years, Volume II: From War to Peace?* (Routledge, 2000).

# Editors and Contributors

**Ben Murane** is the Director of New Generations, where he develops leaders and activists who support the work of the New Israel Fund, the leading funder of Israeli human rights groups, and serves on its board. Murane is also the New York City Co-Chair of Brit Tzedek v'Shalom, the grassroots branch of the pro-Israel, pro-peace movement. He co-publishes Jewschool.com, the largest progressive Jewish blog, and in 2008, he represented Breaking the Silence, an Israeli veterans group exposing human rights abuses. He is the son of a U.S. Army veteran.

**Julia Oestreich** is a doctoral candidate in History at Temple University and the assistant editor at The Jewish Publication Society. After receiving her BA in Government from Smith College, she worked for both the Connecticut and Western Massachusetts branches of the *Jewish Ledger*. She then received her MA in Jewish Communal Service from Gratz College. Oestreich has also worked as a curatorial intern for the National Museum of American Jewish History, an instructor for the Florence Melton Mini-Adult School, and a teaching assistant in the Department of History at Temple University. She is project manager of the *Jewish Choices, Jewish Voices* series.

**Harold Robinson**, rabbi (Hebrew Union College-Jewish Institute of Religion), is the director of the Jewish Welfare Board-Jewish Chaplains Council. He earned a BA from Coe College, and a BHL and MA from Hebrew Union College-Jewish Institute of Religion. In 1999, the College Institute awarded him the Doctorate of Divinity, and in 2005, he received a Doctor of Humane Letters from Coe College. He was rabbi of Temple Israel of Gary, Indiana (1974–1977), the Cape Cod Synagogue (1977–1998), and B'nai Zion Congregation in Shreveport, Louisiana (1998–2006). He has served on the Commission on Social Action, the Resolutions Committee, and the Commission on Religious Living of Reform Judaism. Commissioned an ensign in the U.S. Naval Reserve in 1971, Rear Admiral Robinson received a superseding commission as a chaplain in 1975. In 2000, he was assigned to the Chief of Naval Chaplains Office as Special Assistant for Reserve Manpower, and in 2003, he was promoted to the rank of Rear Admiral and appointed Deputy Chief of Navy Chaplains for Reserve Matters. He has visited our armed forces in Iraq, Afghanistan, Qatar, and Kuwait, and is a Fleet Marine Force-qualified officer. Personal awards include the Distinguished Service Medal, the Legion of Merit, the Meritorious Service Medal, the Naval Commendation Medal with two Gold Stars, and the Navy and Marine Corps Overseas Deployment Ribbon. He retired from the Navy in 2007.

**Joan Schultz** presently serves on the National Executive Committee for the Anti-Defamation League (ADL) and has been involved with the ADL for over 20 years. She is also a long-time active member of the American Israel Public

Affairs Committee (AIPAC). Joan is a realtor in La Jolla, California where she lives with her family.

**Steven Spiegel**, PhD (Harvard University), is professor of political science and director of the Center for Middle East Development at UCLA. He studied international relations and American foreign policy in the Middle East and joined the UCLA faculty in 1966. Since that time he has authored or co-authored over 100 books, articles, and papers and has also written a major international relations textbook, *World Politics in a New Era,* whose fourth edition was published in 2008 by Oxford University Press. Dr. Spiegel provides assistance for Middle East programs at the Institute on Global Conflict and Cooperation of the University of California, San Diego. Through the innovative and informal negotiation techniques he has developed, Dr. Spiegel helps produce cutting-edge ideas for promoting Middle East regional security and cooperation. For this work, he received the Karpf Peace Prize in 1995, awarded to the UCLA professor who has done the most to advance the cause of world peace.

**Rebecca Vilkomerson** is National Director of Jewish Voice for Peace (JVP). She has been a member of JVP since 2002 and is currently an editor of *Jewish Peace News*. Immediately before joining JVP, Rebecca worked for a Palestinian Israel public policy center (DIRASAT) and a Bedouin-Jewish environmental and social justice organization in Israel (BUSTAN). She has over 15 years of experience in community organizing and advocacy campaigns in the United States and Israel. Her study *Public Policy in Divided Societies: The Case for a Civil Rights Institution* was published in July 2008 by Dirasat, the Arab Center for Law and Policy. Vilkomerson is a graduate of Connecticut College and has a MA in Public Policy from Johns Hopkins University.

**Michael Walzer**, PhD (Harvard University), is professor emeritus at the Institute for Advanced Study in Princeton, New Jersey and co-editor of the political-intellectual quarterly *Dissent*. To date, he has written or edited 27 books, including *Just and Unjust Wars: A Moral Argument with Historical Illustrations* (Basic Books, 1977); *Arguing About War* (Yale University Press, 2006); and *Law, Politics, and Morality in Judaism* (Princeton University Press, 2006). Walzer has published over 300 articles, essays, and book reviews in *Dissent, The New Republic, The New York Review of Books, The New Yorker, The New York Times*, and in many scholarly journals.

**Uzi Weingarten**, rabbi (Rabbi Isaac Elchanan Theological Seminary of Yeshiva University), leads seminars in speaking and acting with compassion. He also writes a weekly Torah commentary, emphasizing what we can learn to improve our own human interactions from the text of the Torah and its commentaries.

Editors and Contributors

**Melissa Weintraub,** rabbi (The Jewish Theological Seminary), is the founding co-director of Encounter (www.encounterprograms.org), an educational organization dedicated to providing Jewish leaders from across the political spectrum with exposure to Palestinian life. She is the former director of education at Rabbis for Human Rights-North America, where she authored a number of articles on Jewish law, human dignity, and self-defense.

# Index

## A

Abraham, 60, 104
Abu Ghraib, 36–37, 92, 124–25
Afghanistan, War in, 24–25, 35, 49, 98, 123, 141, 145, 147
airport security, 3, 27, 30–32, 37
Al-Barakaat (Islamic charity org.), 28
Algeria, 123
Allende, Salvador, 22
al-Qaeda, 15, 24, 98
alternative energy sources, 157
Amalek, 53–55, 60
Amir, Yigal, 124
Anti-Defamation League, 31
anti-Israel rhetoric, 34
anti-Semitism, 34
appeasement policies, 34
Arabs, 13, 19, 23–25, 44, 66–68, 82
arms race, 137–38, 145
arms trading, 130, 134, 147–48, 150–57
assassination of terrorists, 16, 18, 40, 68, 89
assembly, right to, 3, 35
asymmetric threats, 150–51

## B

Ba Webe Checkpoint, 42–44
Begin, Menachem, 63
Ben-Gurion, David, 50, 70–71, 93–94
  see also "purity of arms" (tohar ha-neshek) doctrine
bin Laden, Osama, 24–25, 38, 98, 124
Blackwater, 159
blockades, 49, 74
border security, 32, 38, 43–45
Bosnian War, 49
Breaking the Silence (Israel veterans org.), 41–42
Buber, Martin, 104
Bush, George H.W. administration, 155
Bush, George W. administration, 16, 24–25, 45, 119, 155–56
Bybee memo, 125n28

## C

Camp David peace accords, 114
Canaanites, 53–55, 60, 131
captives, 84
Carter, Jimmy, 34
ceasefires, 26, 67
certainty standard (for evaluating threats), 121, 124
checkpoints, 18, 40–45, 68–69
chemical weapons, 82
Cheney, Dick, 161
Chile, 22
China, 150, 152–53
Church Committee reforms, 38
CIA, 158
citizens, responsibilities of, 99, 112–13, 142–44, 149
civilians, 25, 70–71, 73, 76, 86–87, 98–100, 102, 103–4, 108, 110–15
civil liberties
  contemporary sources on, 10–14
  and national security, 3–4, 16–20, 35, 40–46
Clinton administration, 155
cluster bombs, 153–54
coercive interrogation techniques. see torture
Cold War, 75, 140, 146, 159–160
collateral damage, 82, 94, 100
colonialism, 49, 61, 111
conduct of war
  battlefield ethics, 71–72, 81, 94, 99–100, 108–9, 113–15, 120n14
  biblical and rabbinic views on, 83–85
  contemporary sources on, 85–90
  Jewish principles of, 102–3
  in determining just wars, 74, 76–77
  and national values, 67, 91–100, 112, 126, 165
  non-battlefield conduct, 82, 89
  and nuclear/chemical weapons, 74, 82, 89–90
  rape and torture, 81, 96, 106–8, 115, 120n14, 121–24
  see also individual conduct in war
Council of Peace and Security, 44
Cuba, 22, 27–28

180

# Index

## D
Defense Intelligence Agency, 158
defensive wars, 54, 56–57, 70, 73
Department of Homeland Security, 15
Dershowitz, Alan, 37
dignity. *see* human dignity
discipline, 85, 92, 93, 95–99
discretionary wars (*milḥemet reshut*), 54–55, 60–62, 132
discrimination, 93, 95, 99
domestic policy and national security, 27, 31–32, 45, 129, 133, 145–49
draft, 129, 131–37, 140–43
due process, 12, 36, 92, 99–100, 118, 126
Durbin, Richard, 36

## E
economic blockades and boycotts, 49, 74
Egypt, 23, 61–62, 64, 69, 72, 114
Eisenhower, Dwight D., 23, 129, 140–42, 144, 145–49
   *see also* military-industrial complex
email, monitoring of, 3
enemy combatants, 16, 37, 119
ethics
   of arms trading, 151–54, 156–57
   battlefield ethics, 71–72, 81, 94, 99–100, 108–9, 113–15, 120n14
   in foreign and domestic policies, 133, 146–48
   of individual conduct in war, 81, 83–88, 95–99, 105–8, 112–15
   and nuclear proliferation, 154–57
   *see also* "purity of arms" (*tohar ha-neshek*) doctrine

## F
FBI, 122, 158
financial activities, monitoring of, 3, 27–28, 37
foreign policy and arms trading, 152–54
fourth generation warfare. *see* terrorism, responses to
France, 18, 19, 23
free speech, right to, 3, 7–8, 12, 16, 35
Friedman, Thomas, 125

## G
garrison state, 159–60, 165
Gaza, 18, 25–26, 34, 49, 70, 73, 151
Geneva Conventions, 81, 125n28
genocide, 4, 50, 59–60, 75–76
God
   *kevod ha-beriyot* (dignity of created beings), 117–19
   *kinyan ha-kadosh baruch hu* (belonging to God), 119
   man created in His image, 11, 81, 116–17, 167
"Good Samaritan" principle, 120
Great Britain, 18, 19, 21, 23, 36, 65
Grenada, invasion of, 49
Guantanamo Bay detention camp, 37, 45, 116, 122, 125
   *see also* prisoners, rights and dignity of

## H
Halliburton, 159, 161
Hamas, 26–27, 34, 69, 73, 138, 151
*haredi* (Orthodox Jews) exemption, 137
Hawara Checkpoint, 41–42
health care reform, 145, 162
Hezbollah, 34, 57, 69, 110, 138, 151
homeland security, 15–20
hostages, 49, 74, 82
human body, debasing of, 117–18
human dignity, 10, 81, 88, 92, 102–3, 116–19, 126
human life, sanctity of, 31, 102–3, 119–21, 126, 167
humiliation. *see* human dignity
Hussein, Saddam, 93, 107, 109, 150

## I
immigration policies, 3, 31–32
imminent danger principle, 122–24
India, 150, 152, 153, 156
infrastructure, spending on, 162
innocent civilians. *see* civilians
intelligence-gathering techniques, 11–12, 16, 18, 19–20, 37–38, 158–59, 163
internment camps, 3, 16, 36, 40
Intifada, First and Second, 49

# Index

invasions, 22–26, 28, 49–50, 52–53, 75, 91–92
Iran, 27, 34, 69, 138, 150, 154–56, 159
Iraq
    costs of wars, 141
    first war with, 49, 150
    Israel's bombing of nuclear reactor, 73
    and the military-industrial complex, 143–44, 147
    rationale for war with, 109
    sanctions against, 23–24, 74
    second war with, 24–25, 37, 45, 49, 91–93, 101, 105–6, 141–144
    torture in, use of, 123
IRA terrorism, 21
Islamic Jihad, 98, 151
Israel
    arms trading, 130, 151–54
    civil liberties vs. security, 18, 32, 40–46
    and Egypt, 23, 61–62, 64
    and Gaza, 25–26, 30, 34, 49, 70, 73
    *haredi* (authentic Jews) exemption, 137
    Intifada, First and Second, 49
    and Iran, 69, 150
    and Iraq, 34, 73
    Lebanon, wars with, 22, 28, 49, 57, 63, 73, 110
    military-industrial complex, 148
    military service, 137
    national security doctrine, 67–68
    and Palestinians, 18, 19, 22–24, 40–46, 67–69, 77, 110
    peace through strength, 39
    peace treaties, 64, 67, 69
    preemptive actions, 61–62, 72–73
    preventive detention, 18
    "purity of arms" *(tohar ha-neshek)* doctrine, 50, 64, 70–71, 85–86, 93–94
    responses to terrorism, 13, 68–69
    security barriers, 41–44, 68–69
    Six-Day War, 49, 61–62, 64, 68, 72
    and Syria, 150
    torture, use of, 119, 123
    underlying grievances behind terrorism, 22–25
    United Nations' 1947 Partition Resolution, 65–66, 77
    and U.S. security alliance, 138, 148
    vulnerability of, 32, 34
    War of Independence, 49, 66–67, 77
    and West Bank, 25–27, 32, 34, 41–45, 69, 110
    *see also* Palestinians and Palestinian territories
Israel Defense Forces (IDF), 50, 64, 70, 85–86, 93–94, 110
Israel Defense Forces Educational Corps, 41–42
Israeli Supreme Court, 118–19
Italy, 18

## J

Jewish Voice for Peace, 70
Jews, American and the U.S. military, 112–13, 141
Jihadist movement
    anti-Semitic rhetoric, 34
    and profiling, 19
    on September 11, 24
    threats from, 17–19
    *see also* terrorism
Johnson, Lyndon, 141, 145
Jordan, 64, 69

## K

Kahn, Herman, 147
Kennedy, John F., 22
Kennedy, Robert, 22
*kevod ha-beriyot* (dignity of created beings), 117–19
Khalid Sheikh Mohammed, 37
Kibya, 110–15
killing vs. murder, 92
*kinyan ha-kadosh baruch hu* (belonging to God), 119
Korean War, 49, 82, 108, 140
Kuntar, Samir, 110–15
Kuwait, 91–92, 150

## L

landmines, 137–38
law, rule of, 12, 16, 126, 150
Lazarus, Emma, 31
Lebanon
    and Hezbollah, 34, 110, 151
    1982 war, 22, 28, 49, 63
    2006 war, 49, 57, 73, 110, 154
Leibowitz, Yeshayahu, 111–13

# Index

Libya, 155
loyalty to government, 4, 8–10, 167

## M
madrasahs, 32
mandatory wars *(milḥemet mitzvah)*, 54–55, 132
marriage and military exemptions, 131–35
McDonnell Douglas, 159
McVeigh, Timothy, 31
media coverage, 94, 147–48
mercy, 83, 85
*milḥemet hovah* (obligatory wars), 62–63, 132
*milḥemet mitzvah* (mandatory wars), 54–55, 132
*milḥemet reshut* (discretionary wars), 54–55, 60–62, 132
military-industrial complex
    Eisenhower's warning, 129, 140–41, 145–49
    and government spending, 141, 145–46, 159–62
    and national security, 145–49
    and private contractors, 147, 159–61
    profit motive, 139
    U.S.–Israel relations, 148
    *see also* U.S. military
minimum possible harm standard, 121–22
morals. *see* ethics
Morgenthau, Hans, 150
Moveon.org, 36
murder vs. killing, 92
Murtha, John, 36
Muslim-Americans, 35–36
Myanmar, 153

## N
*nakhba* (flight of Palestinian refugees), 77
national security
    and civil liberties, 3–4, 16–20, 35, 40–46
    and domestic policy, 31–32, 129, 133, 145–49
    and the military-industrial complex, 145–49
National Security Agency, 158
*National Strategy for Homeland Security* (White House), 16–17
national values and conduct of war, 91–100, 108–109, 112

neutrality, 62
Niebuhr, Reinhold, 150
non-battlefield conduct, 82, 89
North Korea, 150, 155
nuclear energy, 154–56
Nuclear Non-Proliferation Treaty (1968), 155
nuclear proliferation, 130, 137–38, 154–56, 164
nuclear weapons, 71–73, 74, 82, 89–90

## O
Obama, Barack, 145
Occupied Territories. *see* Palestinians and Palestinian territories
obedience, 5, 8–9, 81, 88–89, 96, 97n4
obligatory wars *(milḥemet hovah)*, 62–63, 132
Office of Financial Assets Control, 27–28
Oklahoma City bombing, 31
Operation Iraqi Freedom, 143–44
    *see also* Iraq
optional wars. *see* discretionary wars *(milḥemet reshut)*

## P
pacifism, 39, 63
Pakistan, 19, 27, 150, 156
Palestinians and Palestinian territories
    civil liberties vs. security, 18, 32, 40–46
    Israel's occupation of, 22–24, 25–27, 69
    militancy of, 68–69
    *nakhba* (flight of Palestinian refugees), 77
    and sovereignty, 75
    *see also* Hamas; Hezbollah
Patriot Act, 45
patriotism. *see* loyalty to government
peace
    biblical and rabbinic views on, 39, 51–52
    contemporary sources on, 55–56
    economic viability of, 164–65
    obligation to seek, xiv, 26, 51, 63, 83, 101–2, 167
    through strength, 39
peace dividend, 161
Petraeus, David, 36
political correctness, 30, 37
political ideology, 36, 45
Powell, Colin, 125n28

# Index

preemptive actions
    biblical and rabbinic views on, 52–53, 61
    contemporary sources on, 55–57
    Israel and, 61–62
    justification for, 72–73
    and self-defense, 50, 94
premeditated acts of violence, 121–22
preventive detention, 16, 18
preventive war. *see* preemptive actions
prisoners,
    rights and dignity of, 118–19
    and torture, 97–98, 108
    treatment of, 96, 99
    *see also* Guantanamo Bay detention camp
privacy, right to, 5–7, 10–13
private contractors, 147, 159–61
private property, 52, 106
profiling, 3, 19–20, 31
prohibited wars, 61–63
propaganda, 94, 136
proportional response, 50, 93, 99
punishment, 121
"purity of arms" *(tohar ha-neshek)* doctrine, 50, 64, 70–71, 85–86, 93–94
pursuer *(rodef)* principle, 120, 124

## Q
Quakers, xi

## R
Rabin, Yitzhak, 64, 124
racial profiling. *see* profiling
rape, 81, 106–7, 115
rapport-building, 122
Reagan, Ronald, 28
renewable energy sources, 157
*rodef* (pursuer) principle, 120, 124
Roosevelt, Franklin Delano, 34

## S
sanctions against Iraq, 23–24, 74
Saudi Arabia, 24, 152–53
Scharff, Hanns Joachim, 99
Schlesinger, Arthur, 22
Scud missile, 34
secession, 49
security barriers, 41–44, 68–69
self-defense
    and just wars, 50, 57, 62
    minimum possible harm standard, 121–22
    as obligation, 120, 167
    and preemptive actions, 50, 94
    and principle of imminent danger, 122
    *see also* "purity of arms" *(tohar ha-neshek)* doctrine
September 11, 3, 15–17, 21–24, 30, 35–36, 45, 150, 162
Sharia Law, 36
Sharon, Ariel, 110–15
Six-Day War, 49, 61–62, 64, 68, 72
Sixth Commandment, 92
Sodom and Gomorrah, 60
soldiers' belief in mission, 143–44
Somalia, 28
South Korea, 150
sovereignty, 65–66, 75–76
Soviet Union, 137, 140, 146, 160
Star Wars, 160–61
Sudan, 153
Suez Canal Crisis, 49
suicide bombings, 32, 43, 150
surveillance
    of financial activities, 3, 27
    legality of, 37
    in public places, 3, 16
    rabbinic views on, 6–7
    as response to terrorism, 31, 45
Syria, 150

## T
Taiwan, 150, 152
targeted bombing, 82
targeted killing, 82, 98–100
technology, 19, 38, 49–50, 94, 137–39, 163–65
telephone calls, monitoring of, 3
terrorism
    and asymmetric threats, 150–51
    contemporary sources on, 12–14
    and military operations, 95, 98, 108

responses to, 3–4, 15–20, 28–29, 40, 68–69, 89
underlying grievances, 21–25
see also Jihadist movement
"ticking bomb" scenario, 37, 98–99, 122–24
*tohar ha-neshek* (purity of arms) doctrine, 50, 64, 70–71, 85–86, 93–94
torture
    Abu Ghraib prisoner abuse, 36–37, 92, 124–25
    and conduct of war, 81–82, 96, 99, 115
    contemporary sources on, 11–12
    dangers of, 124–25
    effectiveness of, 99, 107–8, 121–22
    at Guantanamo Bay detention camp, 116
    in Israel, 119, 123
    Jewish views on, 116–26
    normalization of, 123
    and *rodef* (pursuer) principle, 120n14
treaty obligations, 75, 85, 87
Truman, Harry, 82

# U

United Nations, 38, 65–66, 77
U.S. Army Field Manual, 85
U.S. Department of Homeland Security, 15
U.S. military
    and American Jews, 112–13, 141
    discrimination, 93, 95, 99
    draft, 129, 131–37, 140–43
    hostility toward, 36–37
    intelligence-gathering techniques, 11–12, 16, 18, 19–20, 37–38, 158–59
    oaths of, 96
    proportionality, 50, 93, 99
    research and development, 160–61, 163–64
    spending, 129, 141, 145–46, 159–62
    volunteer army, 36, 129, 136, 142, 163
    see also military-industrial complex

# V

Victims of Arab Terror, 34
video surveillance, 3
Vietnam War, 49, 55–56, 75, 88, 108, 136, 141, 142, 145
visa restrictions, 3, 31–32
volunteer army, 36, 129, 136, 142, 163

# W

*Wall Street Journal*, 23
war
    biblical and rabbinic views on, xiv, 51–54, 83–84, 131–34
    and consensus among the population, 136, 140–43
    contemporary sources on, 54–57, 86–87
    Jewish views on, xi, 39, 101–3, 167
    just wars, 49–50, 62
    types of, 59–63, 69
    see also conduct of war; national security
War of Independence (Israel), 49, 66–67, 77
War on Poverty, 141
waterboarding, 37
weapons technology, 49–50, 69, 94
weapons trade. see arms trading
White Paper, 65
wiretaps. see surveillance, electronic
Wolfowitz, Paul, 24
World War I, 136, 168
World War II, 15, 35, 49, 62, 66, 74, 82, 136, 140, 168

# Y

Yamamoto, Isoroku, 99
Yom Kippur War, 49

# Z

Zionism, 9–10, 59, 64–66